15th Anniversary Quilt, designed, pieced, and quilted by Nancy Taylor

Celebrate
the Tradition
WITH **C&T PUBLISHING**

OVER 70 FABULOUS NEW BLOCKS,
TIPS & STORIES FROM QUILTING'S BEST

Edited by: **Liz Aneloski** and **Joyce Lytle**

C&T PUBLISHING

20TH **ANNIVERSARY**
COLLECTOR'S EDITION

© 2003 C&T Publishing
Founders: Tom and Carolie Hensley
Chief Executive Officer: Todd Hensley
Chief Financial Officer: Tony Hensley
Publisher: Amy Marson
Editor-in-Chief: Darra Williamson
Editor: Liz Aneloski
Technical Editors: Joyce Engels Lytle and Franki Kohler
Copyeditor: Linda Dease Smith
Proofreader: Eva Simoni Erb
Editorial Assistants: Ashlyn Aneloski and Stacy Chamness
Design Director/Cover and Book Designer: Christina D. Jarumay
Illustrator: Tim Manibusan
Production Assistant: Luke Mulks
Full-page Quilt Photography: Sharon Risedorph
Block Photography: Kirstie L. McCormick and Luke Mulks
Published by C&T Publishing, Inc., P.O. Box 1456, Lafayette, California, 94549

Library of Congress Cataloging-in-Publication Data
Celebrate the tradition with C & T Publishing : over 70 fabulous new
blocks, tips & stories from quilting's best / edited by Liz Aneloski and
Joyce Engels Lytle.– 20th anniversary collector's ed.
     p. cm.
  ISBN 1-57120-215-3 (paper trade)
  1. Quilting. 2. Patchwork 3. C & T Publishing. I. Aneloski, Liz.
II. Lytle, Joyce Engels. III. Title.
  TT835.C415 2003
  746.46–dc21
                                    2003007609

Printed in China
10 9 8 7 6 5 4 3 2 1

Dedication

From Carolie and Tom:

To the many people who had faith in Roberta, Tom, and me when all hope was down. To Tony and Todd for carrying on the tradition of publishing the best quality quilting books in the world. To the wonderful staff at C&T that creates magic. Follow your dreams—they will come true.

—CAROLIE AND TOM HENSLEY

From Tony and Todd:

To our parents, Tom and Carolie Hensley, for taking a big risk and saying, "We can do that." Your honesty and work ethic are an inspiration and a guiding light.

To Jennifer and Julie, who are always there for us.

To the talented and creative authors who have brought their life's work to C&T and trusted us with presenting their vision in a printed presentation. Without you, there would be no C&T Publishing.

To the exceptional staff and freelance partners of C&T, both past and present, for your outstanding contributions to the creative process.

To shop owners around the world who have followed their dreams and made quilting and fiber arts a stable and growing industry.

—TODD AND TONY HENSLEY

In Memoriam

In the fall of 1992 Louise Owens Townsend left *Quilters Newsletter Magazine* as managing editor to become a book editor at C&T. Citing her desire to move to northern California and make a change in her life, Louise packed her bags and moved to the San Francisco Bay Area.

Louise contributed to the success of C&T. In addition to her keen eye and wonderful humor, she brought a feeling of confidence to C&T. With our goals set on improving our quality and increasing our book output, Louise helped make that transition a smooth one.

On October 4, 1995 Louise Owens Townsend lost her 10-year battle with cancer. She was 53.

Everyone at C&T Publishing is honored to have had the opportunity to work with her. She is missed by all who knew her.

Contents

The Beginnings
—You Publish What!??

"Thank you for the opportunity to review your business proposal. Unfortunately, we are unable to approve your loan. We wish you the best of luck in your endeavors."

These were the words we heard from more than one bank when we set out to establish C&T Publishing and publish our first book.

So . . . how did C&T come to be?

Early in 1983, Roberta Horton, a popular local quilt instructor, was teaching a class on Amish quilts at The Cotton Patch, Carolie's quilt shop in Lafayette, California. One day, Roberta mentioned to Carolie that she wanted to write a book on Amish quilts and did not yet have a publisher.

Carolie quickly replied, "Roberta, we will do that!" In Carolie's mind this would be no problem. How hard could it be to publish a book? That evening, she presented the idea to husband Tom. "Roberta has a manuscript for a book on Amish quilts, and she wants us to publish it for her."

"What?!" Tom responded. "I don't know how to be a publisher!"

"Go to the library," Carolie replied.

So Tom was off to the local library in search of information. He found a book by Dan Poynter, *The Self-Publishing Manual*, which he read several times from cover to cover, each time becoming more intrigued by the possibilities. Next, he enrolled in a course in publishing at University of California at Berkeley, and determined it would take an initial investment of $25,000 to publish Roberta's book.

The next challenge was figuring out where to find $25,000! First stop: the local bank—and you know what they said. Seems they didn't like the idea of having 10,000 copies of a book in their lobby (since the print run of books would be used as collateral for the loan).

Rather than being dejected, Carolie and Tom became more determined than ever to prove the banks wrong. They set out to find ten friends willing to invest $2,500 each to launch the book. Thanks to Alice Hoskins, Barbara Weirick, Cathie Hoover, Ulf and Susan Dalhgren, Howard and Margy Nickelson, Betty Kisby, William and Jean Fredeking, Susan McNally, Irene Shirar, Kathy Dimond, and Eleanor Maharry (Carolie's mom), the $25,000 was raised within two weeks, a limited partnership was created, and a new publishing company was born. Of course, the fledgling company needed a name, and—in case you haven't guessed—they chose C&T for Carolie and Tom.

With that part of their mission accomplished, the new publishers could now focus on bringing the dream of Roberta's book to reality.

In fall 1983, Carolie, Tom, and their debut author (Roberta) went to Quilt Market in Houston with little more than a printed book cover and a photocopy of the book pasted inside. They took enough orders to cover their expenses, and headed home to finish the book and begin shipping.

Before long, 10,000 copies of *An Amish Adventure* were delivered from the printer directly to "company headquarters"— Carolie and Tom's home! Garage, living room, and even bedrooms were converted to warehouse boxes of books. Shipping materials, labels, tape, and blank invoices were purchased.

Now life *really* changed in the Hensley household! Tom came home from work and spent his evenings packing orders, while Carolie typed invoices and took books to the post office for shipment the next day.

An Amish Adventure was selling very well. C&T Publishing was shipping books all over the United States. The partners were receiving quarterly checks, and eventually recovered their initial investments and more. The partnership was dissolved. To keep the momentum going—and to make C&T's order form look more impressive—Carolie and Tom decided to distribute Barbara Johannah's book, *The Quick Quiltmaking Handbook.*

From 1984 to 1987, C&T added several more titles. In addition to two new books by Roberta—*Stained Glass Quilt Techniques* and *Calico & Beyond*—C&T published books by Judith Baker Montano, Becky Schaefer, Pepper Cory, Jeffrey Gutcheon, Blanche Young, Helen Young, Katie Pasquini Masopust, Marianne Fons, Liz Porter, Jean Wells, Harriet Hargrave, and Judy Mathieson.

C & T PUBLISHING
P.O. Box 1456
LAFAYETTE, CA 94549

(415) 937-0605

C&T's first letterhead. The logo changed from cats to horse and buggy.

C & T PUBLISHING

P.O. Box 1456
LAFAYETTE, CA 94596

(415) 937-0605

C&T Publishing's first business card. Note Carolie's love for cats.

AN AMISH ADVENTURE
A Workbook for Color in Quilts
by Roberta Horton
• Color Photographs • Diagrams
• Detailed Explanations
C&T Publishing
P.O. Box 1456,.Lafayette, CA 94549
*Price: $12.95 plus $1.50 postage
California Residents add sales tax*

C&T's first advertisement for *An Amish Adventure* as seen in *Quilters Newsletter Magazine*

The return trip from Quilt Market 1984 when the trailer of books hit black ice.

Tom picking up the mess of books and supplies.

Spring Quilt Market 1991. Diane Pedersen sets up the C&T booth.

Spring Quilt Market 1991. The booth all finished and ready for opening day.

Fall Quilt Market 1992. Authors Margaret Peters and Elly Sienkiewicz sign books for shop owners and teachers.

Spring Quilt Market 1992. From left to right: Jon Hofioni, Tony Hensley, and Tom Hensley take a moment from writing orders to pose for the camera.

Staff meeting and pizza party at C&T. From left to right: Liz Aneloski, Tom Hensley, Todd Hensley, Harold Nadel, Wendy Schmidt, Joe Schmidt, Jon Hofioni, Joyce Lytle (standing), Louise Townsend.

Fall Quilt Market 1993. C&T's 10-year anniversary celebration.

Karey Bresenhan presents Tony Hensley with a best booth award at Spring Quilt Market 1994.

Tony Hensley, Carolie Hensley, Tom Hensley, Todd Hensley during Quilt Market.

Todd (left) and Tony Hensley celebrate the opening of C&T's new office facility in 1997.

Eventually the house filled floor to ceiling with boxes upon boxes of books. Sons Tony and Todd both recall returning from college to find their bedrooms overtaken with boxes. Navigating from room to room resembled running a maze.

Todd joined the company full time in 1988, and—with Tony—helped move the operations out of the house and into an office and warehouse facility. Finally, the house was back to normal! At the time, the warehouse seemed enormous, but within a few years C&T was again bursting at the seams.

By the time 1990 rolled around, Tony had joined the company full time as well and Diane Pedersen was hired as C&T's first full-time employee. Carolie and Tom decided it was time to let go of the reins, and agreed to sell C&T to Tony and Todd.

The brothers realized a few keys for success that they continue to espouse:

▧ Maintain the highest standard of quality for all C&T books and products.

▧ Employ creative and thoughtful people who appreciate quilting and fiber arts.

▧ Publish the work of talented authors who are experts in their field.

▧ Make decisions based on doing the right thing and treating people the right way.

Since its beginnings in 1983, C&T has built an extensive list of best-selling titles that continue to set the industry standard.

This would never have been possible without the untiring effort of the C&T employees, freelancers, and authors. Thank you to Roberta Horton, the initial investors, and to everyone who has been a part of the C&T success story. It has been one amazing journey . . .

. . . and happily, the best is yet to come!

Carolie Hensley
Tom Hensley
Tony Hensley
Todd Hensley

Designed by Liz Aneloski, pieced by Joyce Lytle and Liz Aneloski, quilted by Joyce Lytle and Elke Torgerson

20 Years of

Roberta Horton

FAVORITE C&T STORY

I was C&T's first author. I had been teaching an Amish quilt series for several years. *An Amish Adventure: A Workbook for Color in Quilts* was essentially put together in about a month. I would write a chapter and do rough sketches. When I dropped these off at the designer, I would see the previous chapter, which included the corrections of the copy editor plus the finished illustrations for my approval. FAST.

I remember flying on the plane to the Houston Quilt Market with my publisher, Tom Hensley, to introduce the book. The book was being printed as we flew. We amused ourselves looking at the photocopied version of the book. At Market, Tom rented a chair in someone else's booth. He and I took turns sitting in the chair as we sold the book. C&T was born!

 Favorite QUILTING TIP

DON'T OVERMATCH YOUR FABRICS. EXCITEMENT IS GENERATED WHEN THE COLORS ARE SLIGHTLY DIFFERENT FROM EACH OTHER, THE PATTERNS DIFFERENT IN SCALE AND SUBJECT MATTER. IN OTHER WORDS—MISMATCH.

Judith Baker Montano

Favorite QUILTING TIP

WE OFTEN FORGET THE STRUGGLE TO LEARN A NEW TECHNIQUE, AND WE DO NOT SEE THE PROGRESS AND CHANGES IN OUR WORK THROUGHOUT THE YEARS.

PROUDEST C&T EXPERIENCE

I have been working in the quilting and needlework industry since 1985, and one of the things I am most proud of is that I started with C&T Publishing over breakfast and a handshake!

I met Tom and Carolie Hensley at the 1985 Quilt Market in Houston and asked them if they would be interested in a book about crazy quilting. We agreed to meet the next morning for breakfast. By the end of our meal I had made up my mind to cancel the two meetings booked with other publishers and the Hensleys decided to take a chance and publish my book. Our only contract was a handshake and a verbal agreement. It was the beginning of a long friendship and business relationship.

Roberta Horton

1983

Roberta Horton
Stained Glass Quilting Technique

1984

Becky Schaefer
WORKING IN MINIATURE
A MACHINE PIECING APPROACH TO MINIATURE QUILTS

1984

C&T Authors
THE STARS SPEAK

Jean and Valori Wells

JEAN'S FAVORITE QUILTING STORY

Little did I know that when I asked my daughter Valori—who was in art school at the time—to do the garden photography for *Everything Flowers* that she would become interested in quilting. The next year we worked on another book, *Through the Garden Gate*; she made her first quilt, *My Mother's Garden*. I had given her and a friend a mini-lesson in quiltmaking, and she took to the stitch-and-flip technique that you use for foundation-pieced crazy quilts. She saw all these other possibilities for design. I was so surprised to receive the quilt in the mail from her, and totally amazed by the design and construction.

JEAN'S PROUDEST C&T AND QUILTING EXPERIENCES

Working with my daughter in the Stitchin' Post and on books has been a joy, one that I certainly didn't anticipate. We are a great team and both contribute different ways on our projects. Sending her to art school was a bonus. Our love of gardens and quilting has led us into many projects relating to quilts with a flare for nature.

Favorite QUILTING TIP

TAKE YOUR COLOR CLUES FROM MOTHER NATURE. OBSERVE WHAT YOU SEE AROUND YOU. TAKE A SNAPSHOT WITH YOUR MIND, OR A PICTURE WITH YOUR CAMERA. IF YOU LIKE THAT PICTURE, USE THE COLORS IN THE SAME PROPORTIONS IN THE QUILT AND IT WILL WORK. IT DOESN'T MATTER WHAT THE QUILT DESIGN IS.

WHEN VALORI IS PLANNING A QUILT DESIGN, THE QUILTING IS PART OF THE OVERALL PLAN FROM THE VERY BEGINNING. WHEN YOU PIECE, YOU SIMPLIFY, THEN THE QUILTING IS ADDING IN THE DESIGN LINES AND UNIFYING THE IDEA.

Roberta Horton

1985

Judith Baker Montano

1986

Katie Pasquini

1986

Jean Wells

1987

Blanche Young

FAVORITE C&T STORY

My proudest achievement is my book *Tradition With A Twist*, co-authored with my daughter Dalene Young Stone. The continued success of the book, along with the stories of quilters and students who have shown me their quilts and pictures of quilts made using the book, have provided me with great satisfaction.

Also, I am especially proud of the fact that three of my daughters have worked with me on books for C&T. I never really taught them to sew, they were just always surrounded by it, absorbed it, and have become talented and creative quiltmakers.

SIGNIFICANT CHANGES IN THE LAST 20 YEARS

In my opinion, it is the acceptance of machine quilting.

 *Favorite* QUILTING TIP

WHEN I SWEEP MY SEWING ROOM, I PUT A SMALL PIECE OF BATTING AT THE BOTTOM OF THE BROOM; IT WILL STICK, AND WHEN I SWEEP, IT EASILY PICKS UP STRAY PINS AND NEEDLES ALONG WITH THREADS AND SMALL SCRAPS OF FABRIC!

FAVORITE QUILTING QUOTE

IN TEACHING, NOT A CLASS GOES BY THAT I DON'T HAVE AT LEAST ONE STUDENT THAT IS AFRAID OF MAKING A MISTAKE, OR AFRAID THAT THEIR WORK IS NOT PERFECT. I ASSURE THEM, "THE MYSTICAL CRITICAL QUILT COMMITTEE IS NOT INVITED."

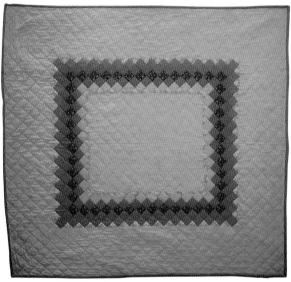

Early Quilt

Recent Quilt

Pepper Cory

Blanche Young & Helen Young Frost

Blanche Young & Helen Young Frost

1987

Helen Young Frost

FAVORITE QUILTING STORY

I began teaching quiltmaking when I was in my early twenties, so I was usually much younger than my students. Once I was showing one of my more elderly students how she should sew a certain block when she put me in my place. "Girl," she said, "I've been quilting longer than you've been living!" Now, at the beginning of a class, I have everyone introduce herself and tell how long she's been quilting.

PROUDEST C&T EXPERIENCE

In 1987, I was hired by C&T to illustrate Judy Mathieson's first Mariner's Compass book. That summer I was pregnant with my son, Paul, and it was a real race to see if I could finish the drawings before he made his appearance! I did, and as a special thank you, Judy made me a wonderful Mariner's Compass wall quilt.

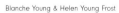 *Favorite* **QUILTING TIP**

USE A SMALL WOODEN COCKTAIL FORK, RATHER THAN A STILETTO OR YOUR FINGER, TO GUIDE SEAMS UNDER THE PRESSER FOOT WHILE MACHINE PIECING. THE WOOD HOLDS THE FABRIC AND CANNOT DAMAGE THE THROAT PLATE LIKE A METAL STILETTO CAN.

Jeffrey Gutcheon

Favorite **QUILTING TIP**

OIL YOUR MACHINE AT LEAST ONCE EVERY 3000 MILES.

SIGNIFICANT CHANGES IN THE LAST 20 YEARS

There now seems to be less inclination to work in plain colors and less interest in making traditional piecework quilts than formerly. Maybe time is more precious and budgets are tighter than they used to be, but the sacrifice is a lot of creative potential.

Blanche Young & Helen Young Frost

Marianne Fons

Jeffrey Gutcheon

Judy Mathieson

1987

Judy Mathieson

PROUDEST C&T EXPERIENCE

C&T, a very new company at the time, was brave enough to trust my ideas and me and publish a book about Mariner's Compass designs. I think the general feeling about quilters is often that they will only buy books about quick and easy stuff. There proved to be great depth among quiltmakers and they were interested in the book then and continued to be interested in 1996 when C&T published a new updated version.

SIGNIFICANT CHANGES IN THE LAST 20 YEARS

I have watched the quilt community and the industry that serves it for over 25 years. I remember wanting to buy every book that came out because there had been so little published information when I began. Now, I can pick and choose among the variety available.

The most significant changes in products, after fabric and books, are the rotary cutters and related tools. However, for my work, the greatest impact has been the rediscovery of very old techniques—paper and foundation piecing. I find it fascinating that an old technique intended to use up small scraps should be so valuable to contemporary quilters.

Mary Mashuta

FAVORITE C&T STORY

When I was making quilts and samples for one of my books, Carolie Hensley gave me a printed-rose feed sack that belonged to her mother-in-law. I used it to make an apron pictured in *Cotton Candy Quilts*. I kept hoping Todd would discover the picture one day, but finally I had to tell him to look on page 69.

Favorite QUILTING TIP

BREAK THE HABIT OF PULLING THE SPOOL OFF THE SPINDLE OF A THREADED SEWING MACHINE WHEN YOU ARE READY TO CHANGE COTTON THREAD, BECAUSE YOU DEPOSIT EXCESS FUZZ IN THE TENSION MECHANISM, WHICH HASTENS IT BEING OUT OF BALANCE. INSTEAD, CUT THE THREAD AT THE SPOOL AND THEN PULL THE PIECE ON DOWN THROUGH THE MACHINE UNTIL IT IS FREE. KNOT THE END AS IT COMES OFF AND LOOP THE THREAD AROUND TWO FINGERS. THE THREAD IS READY AND JUST THE RIGHT LENGTH FOR THE NEXT TIME YOU NEED SOME BASTING THREAD!

Susan McKelvey

Katie Pasquini

Blanche Young & Helen Young Frost

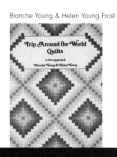

Blanche Young & Helen Young Frost

1988

Marianne Fons

FAVORITE C&T STORY

I went to Quilt Market in Houston to promote *Fine Feathers* in 1987. The C&T booth consisted of one table, and two chairs. Tom and either I or Pepper Cory occupied the chairs. The table decoration was an artificial flower arrangement. We wrote out orders by hand. Todd was there to take a look at the quilting world. He was in college and studied where he could. (There must have been a third chair for him.)

PROUDEST C&T EXPERIENCE

It has been wonderful to watch the growth of C&T, owned and operated by fantastic people. My books are out of print now, but I am still proud to have been an author for C&T.

 Favorite QUILTING TIP

IT TAKES A LONG TIME TO FINISH A QUILT WHEN YOU'RE NOT WORKING ON IT!

Liz Porter

SIGNIFICANT CHANGES IN THE LAST 20 YEARS

I feel the biggest change has been the growing acceptance of machine quilting, particularly work done on longarm quilting machines. Quilting on these machines has risen from the "mattress pad" variety to what is in many cases true artistry. The many professional machine quilters are allowing all of us to complete our UFOs into finished quilts in a timely manner.

Jean Wells & Marina Anderson

Marianne Fons & Liz Porter

Mary Mashuta

Elly Sienkiewicz

1988   1988   1989   1989

Jane Hall

FAVORITE QUILTING QUOTE

From Beth Gutcheon, *The Perfect Patchwork Primer*: "Patchwork is a craft born of the hardest necessity . . . Patchwork is really the blues of the American woman."

FAVORITE C&T STORY

When *Perfect Pineapples* came out, my partner Dixie Haywood and I were at Quilt Market (1989) and sat in the C&T booth all day demonstrating our foundation piecing techniques. We had a great time, and the best of all was the night the entire group went to a fabulous barbecue place, with Tom and Carolie Hensley. I also remember Todd's and Diane Pedersen's help and encouragement as we worked on our first book.

PROUDEST QUILTING EXPERIENCE

What I am proud of in my quilting experience is my involvement in the quilt world—writing books with Dixie, traveling around the country teaching and lecturing, and meeting an incredible variety of people who share my passion for quilting in whatever form. (I have, of course, also loved showing my quilts, having them pictured in magazines, and winning awards.)

 Favorite QUILTING TIP

Use foundations for piecing EVERYTHING! They provide stability and an incredible precision, even with the simplest patterns.

Dixie Haywood

SIGNIFICANT CHANGES IN THE LAST 20 YEARS

I think the most significant change in the last twenty years is the explosion of companies geared toward quilting. Also, the increased professionalism of those who started quilting because they loved the process and went on to have a place in the wider quilt world. What largely *hasn't* changed is the generous support and sharing among most quilters and their envy-free recognition of the pleasure in each other's fine work. (We all, of course, have a nanosecond of wishing we had thought of it, and/or were capable of making it!)

FAVORITE QUILTING QUOTE

One of the husbands was helping us hang our first quilt show. As the quilts were going up on the frames, he turned to his wife and said, "So *that's* what a finished quilt looks like!"

A second, more prescient, quote came from my supportive husband when I first started teaching, writing, and accepting commissions. When I told him that our life would get back to normal when I finished the big project I was working on, he replied, "You may as well face the fact that this *is* normal." All too true . . .

Jane Hall & Dixie Haywood

1989

Pepper Cory

1989

Susan McKelvey

1990

Pepper Cory

1990

Quilt San Diego

PROUDEST C&T EXPERIENCE

Quilt Visions is proudest of its success in promoting the quilt as art through its exhibitions and publication of the accompanying catalogs. C&T has played an important part in our success through its production of catalogs for several Quilt Visions exhibits.

SIGNIFICANT CHANGES IN THE LAST 20 YEARS

We at Quilt Visions feel that one of the most significant changes in quilting in the last 20 years is the acceptances of the quilt as art and the increased quality, interest, value, and respect gained by art quilts over that time.

Harriet Hargrave

PROUDEST QUILTING EXPERIENCE

The thing that I am most proud of, and the greatest hurdle in my quiltmaking experience, is the revolution in quiltmaking that I started with the introduction of "heirloom-style" machine quilting in the very early 1980s. I can remember the looks of disapproval and dismay, that I was publicly promoting machine quilting our quilt tops. I coined the term "hand quilting with an electric needle" to ease the tension, and very soon people were catching on. When I walk through Quilt Market now, almost everything is machine quilted. I had no idea when I showed my quilts in the beginning that we would achieve so much in such a short time.

FAVORITE QUILTING EXPERIENCE

My favorite quilting experience is every time I teach a beginners' machine quilting class and see the excitement in the students as they discover that THEY CAN DO IT! If I do nothing but instill good technique and workmanship in my students, I will feel I have accomplished everything.

Quilt San Diego

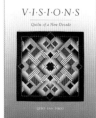

Elly Sienkiewicz

Roberta Horton

Harriet Hargrave

1990

Jean Ray Laury

FAVORITE QUILTING STORY

I once participated in a fundraising event where I was given a small booth space in which to display my work. Ticket holders were invited to take a look at the work, watch demos, nibble on goodies, and visit with the artists and writers.

A woman approached my booth, looked for a bit, and then (without even a smile or a hello) snapped, "How much is that quilt?"

I told her that piece wasn't for sale, to which she barked, "That's what they always say. Just tell me your price."

"I'm sorry," I repeated, "but the piece isn't for sale." She stalked off. A few minutes later she returned and demanded again to know the price. When I repeated my comment she said "Well what do you think you're going to do with it if you don't sell it to me?"

Ordinarily it takes me a day to think of the comeback I want, but I next heard this coming out of my mouth: "Well, I'm just going to sit here and when someone comes along that I really like, I might just give it to her."

She walked off, absorbing my message. And it clarified for me the importance we attach to finding good homes for our work. It is so easy to give quilts to friends or family. It's often hard to sell them. We always hope to find the person who will appreciate what we have put into the piece . . . the time, love, frustration, passion, and pleasure.

Early Quilt

Recent Quilt

Joen Wolfrom

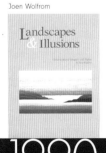

Jean Wells & Marina Anderson

Judith Baker Montano

Elly Sienkiewicz

1990   1990   1991   1991

Margaret Peters

SIGNIFICANT CHANGES IN THE LAST 20 YEARS

I first entered the quilting industry as a sales rep. I had the glorious job of selling quilting products to quilting shops. To think that I am writing this now is unbelievable. The changes I have seen in the past 20 years have been something I would not have missed for the world. The friends I have made and the changing life experiences have been the most exciting journey I have ever taken.

I can remember when there were no more than a dozen pattern companies and even fewer quilt book publishers. The first I heard of C&T Publishing was in Carolie Hensley's store, The Cotton Patch. She told me she and her husband Tom were going to publish a book by Roberta Horton, *An Amish Adventure*. I remember when they started the company. It was in their living room, soon taking over the whole house. Their sons, Todd and Tony, who now own and operate C&T Publishing, have had to move the company to larger quarters, twice.

This growth has happened with the fabric companies, too. When I started, they were not really interested in "quilters." Today, they cater to the quilting industry as it continues to be one of the fastest growing industries in America. With sewing machine companies, the change has been striking. Twenty-five years ago, you bought a sewing machine that stitched forward and backward and made buttonholes, and you were ready to

dress the world. Check out any sewing machine today; the promoted feature will be the quilting capabilities of that machine. The makers of cloth dolls and quilted garments have now become a large presence in the industry, also.

I have never regretted my more than 25 years in quiltmaking and all that it has done for me. Designing a Christmas tree for the Smithsonian, being invited to the White House, experiencing the thrill of being asked to write books for C&T, teaching, and speaking all over the U.S., all of this I owe to this incredible industry. And I have been able to meet some of the world's greatest living artists. What a journey it has been.

Elly Sienkiewicz
APPLIQUÉ EASY WAYS!
1991

Pepper Cory
HAPPY TRAILS
1991

Harriet Hargrave
Mastering Machine Appliqué
1992

Jean Wells
Memorabilia Quilting
1992

Margaret Peters
CHRISTMAS TRADITIONS
1992

Diana McClun

FIRST-QUILT EXPERIENCE

Our home was in a small, rural, south-eastern Idaho town where long winters meant lots of bed quilts, and my doll bed was no exception. At the age of five, with early inspirations from my mother and grandmothers, I made my first quilt for my dollies, using our new Singer sewing machine. The 1930s fabrics were leftover scraps from housedresses and aprons, found in the scrap drawer. I adored those fabrics, purchased at the local J.C. Penney store, and would play for hours combining colors and patterns.

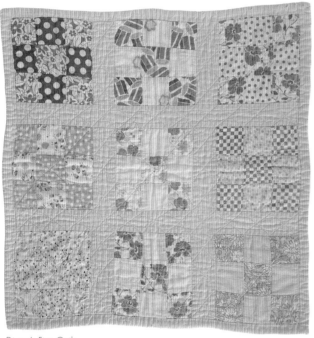

Diana's First Quilt

Diana and Laura's Recent Quilt

Jean Wells

Jean Wells

Jean Wells

Jean Wells

1992

Laura Nownes

FIRST-QUILT EXPERIENCE

I loved the quilting process, and knew immediately it was something I wanted to pursue. Little did I know at the time what an exciting path I had ventured onto. It has been a creative and rewarding experience.

PROUDEST QUILTING EXPERIENCE

I am very proud to be able to share my passion for quiltmaking though teaching. Over the past 20 years I have worked with over 3000 wonderful students, instructing them in the basics of quiltmaking, and enabling them to become lifelong quiltmakers.

Laura's First Quilt

Diana and Laura's Recent Quilt

Quilt San Diego

Katie Pasquini Masopust

Elly Sienkiewicz

Joen Wolfrom

1992

Doreen Speckmann

IN MEMORIAM:
C&T Publishing and the entire quilting community were saddened by the news that Doreen Speckmann, quilt artist and C&T author, passed away on September 18, 1999.

Doreen was a highly accomplished quilt teacher and designer. Her quilts are famous as innovative adaptations of traditional patterns, built upon a series of component blocks that often create the illusion of curves from straight piecing. She taught throughout the world on her quilting cruises and international quilters' tours.

Doreen was a wonderful teacher who was loved by quilters all over the world. C&T Publishing remembers Doreen as an enthusiastic, vibrant friend who lived exuberantly. She touched many quilters with her colorful quilts, entertaining stories, and hilarious sense of humor. She is deeply missed by everyone in the quilting world.

Sally Collins

Favorite **QUILTING TIP**
MEASURE YOUR WORK AS YOU SEW.

FAVORITE QUILTING STORY
Back in the early 1990s I was invited to teach at Empty Spools Quilt Conference at Asilomar for the very first time. Actually, it was my very first "BIG" teaching assignment, and I was excited beyond words and scared to death, all at the same time. I was worried if anyone would sign up for my class, and then worried if I could put together a week-long class that would hold up to the reputation of this conference. I worried about everything! After arriving, I then wondered what I was doing there and felt very isolated and like an outsider. I did not know the other teachers and I'm not very extroverted, so I felt quite alone on that first day. Then something wonderful happened. Roberta Horton so very kindly invited me to breakfast. Yes, THE Roberta Horton. She offered suggestions, answered questions, and alleviated my fears . . . in short, she made me feel as if I belonged at Asilomar and a part of the quilt community. I will be forever grateful for her kindness and how it made me feel. As a result, whenever I am at a conference or anywhere where I meet up with a newcomer, I always try to be kind, offer any help I can, and attempt to make her feel a part of things. Thank you, Roberta.

FAVORITE QUILTING QUOTE
YOU DON'T HAVE TO BE RIGHT THE FIRST TIME, JUST THE LAST TIME.

Jean Ray Laury

1992

Mary Mashuta

1992

Doreen Speckmann

1993

Judith Baker Montano

1993

Judith Baker Montano
1993

Shirley Nilsson

FAVORITE QUILTING EXPERIENCE

I was scheduled to teach an all-day workshop at a church facility. We arrived just in time to see a man on a ladder reach out with a large pair of wire cutters and cut through the main incoming electric cable! Calming myself, I quietly asked him, "Was that the electricity to this part of the facility?"

"Yes it was, Ma'am." he replied.

"Oh no!" I exploded, "I have 32 students and their sewing machines arriving shortly to attend an all-day workshop!"

"Are you sure?" he replied, "I was hired to redo the whole electrical system and it will take at least two days to complete."

So off we went to the office and discovered that someone had made a mistake and had booked the electrical redo and the workshop for the same day.

"Let me see what I can do," the resourceful electrician said. He scurried off and in no time returned with a bunch of friends, carrying armloads of heavy-duty cords. Thank you to the Arizona electrician who saved the day!

SIGNIFICANT CHANGES IN THE LAST 20 YEARS

The most significant change I have observed is the gradual acceptance of fabric as a valid art medium.

When I first started making my "soft pictures" and entered them in art shows, they were summarily rejected. Today my soft pictures are accepted and have hung in galleries and art shows in the U.S. and Canada. Beautiful original-design quilts and wallhangings today hang next to oil paintings, acrylics, and watercolors in galleries all over the world. We in the fabric art world can rejoice in the recognition, but we must also continue our quiet crusade to gain total acceptance as a valid art form.

Shirley Nilsson

Jean Wells

Jean Wells

Jean Wells

Jean Wells

1993

Miriam Gourley

🔸 *Favorite* QUILTING TIP

USE A DRYER SHEET TO SMOOTH OVER THREAD BEFORE HAND STITCHING. THIS HELPS PREVENT TANGLES AND KNOTS.

FAVORITE QUILTING EXPERIENCE

A few years ago, I accompanied my friend, Robin, on a quilt-hunting expedition. She and I were able to see many beautiful antique quilts, and she picked one that I especially liked. It was an Around the World patterned quilt, made with pastels in the 1920s. Imagine my surprise when it arrived in a box on my doorstep, as her gift to me! This certainly is my favorite of several beloved quilts in my collection.

Yvonne Porcella

FAVORITE QUILTING QUOTE

WHILE CUTTING MY FABRIC SELECTIONS, A QUILT STORE EMPLOYEE STATED, "YOU DO KNOW THESE FABRICS DON'T GO TOGETHER." OOPS. I WAS BUYING EXTRA FABRICS TO COMPLETE AN IN-PROGRESS PROJECT.

🔸 *Favorite* QUILTING TIPS

A 15" X 15" OMNIGRID RULER IS WONDERFUL TO USE TO SQUARE UP A BLOCK.

I HAVE TWO OF EVERY TOOL IN MY STUDIO; ROTARY CUTTERS, SCISSORS, TEMPLATE SIZES, RULER SIZES, PENS, MARKERS, AND SO ON, BUT ONLY ONE SEWING MACHINE. WHEN IT BREAKS OR THE TIMING IS OFF, I WISH I HAD TWO SEWING MACHINES, TOO!

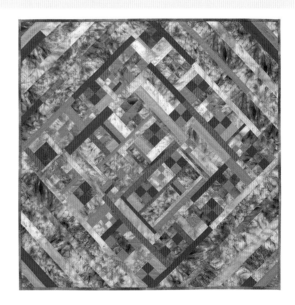

Miriam Gourley

Diana McClun & Laura Nownes

Susan McKelvey

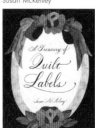

Elly Sienkiewicz

1993

Alex Anderson

FAVORITE QUILTING EXPERIENCE

There are so many facets of quilting that I enjoy, it would be hard to pick just one exact moment. But early in my quilting experience (fifteen-plus years ago) I can remember the day I completed a really large, intricately quilted piece. Before I took it off the frame, my son (aged five or six at the time) and I held hands and danced around it. Upon completion of each quilt I still experience the same joy. I just can't seem to get my son to dance with me around the frame any more.

SIGNIFICANT CHANGES IN THE LAST 20 YEARS

Quilting is no longer just woman's art. It has crossed genders and generations and is continuing to grow. It is a very exciting time to be a quilter, and I have the honor of watching people fall in love with the craft as I have.

Favorite QUILTING TIP

WHEN THREADING A NEEDLE, CUT THE THREAD ON AN ANGLE (DO NOT MOISTEN), WET THE OPPOSITE SIDE OF THE HOLE OF THE NEEDLE AND THE THREAD WILL POP RIGHT THROUGH THE HOLE.

Jinny Beyer

Favorite QUILTING TIP

SPRING AND AUTUMN ARE THE TIMES OF YEAR TO TAKE A NEW LOOK AT THE COLORS AROUND YOU. A COUPLE OF YEARS AGO I WENT INTO MY GARDEN IN EARLY APRIL AND PICKED SOME OF THE SPRING FLOWERS. I SCANNED THEM INTO THE COMPUTER AND WAS ABLE TO ISOLATE ALL OF THE WONDERFUL COLORS. IF YOU LOOK AT THE COLORS FOUND IN FLOWERS, YOU WILL SEE THAT NO SINGLE COLOR STANDS ALONE. THERE IS NOT JUST ONE YELLOW, BUT SEVERAL DIFFERENT YELLOW TONES. FURTHERMORE, ONE COLOR SHADES SUBTLY INTO ANOTHER. I KEEP IN MIND WHAT I SEE IN NATURE WHEN PLANNING COLOR SCHEMES FOR QUILTS. I SELECT THE MAIN COLORS I WANT TO USE AND THEN FIND WHATEVER OTHER COLORS I NEED TO ALLOW ME TO SHADE ALL OF THOSE COLORS TOGETHER. YOU WILL BE SURPRISED AT SOME OF THE COLORS THAT ARE NECESSARY TO SHADE FROM ONE COLOR TO ANOTHER, IT IS THE DIRTIER, DULLER, "OFF" COLORS THAT MAKE ALL THE OTHERS WORK. THE MORE VARIETIES OF COLORS YOU USE IN YOUR QUILTS WITH SUBTLE SHADING FROM ONE COLOR TO ANOTHER, THE MORE YOU WILL BE ABLE TO APPROXIMATE THE BEAUTY AROUND YOU.

Kathy Pace

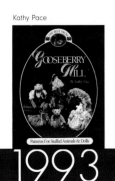

1993

Jean Wells

1993

Jean Ray Laury

1994

Margaret Peters

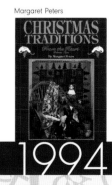

1994

Valerie Hearder

PROUDEST C&T EXPERIENCE

I have been making quilts for 30 years and my teaching and writing career has brought so many wonderful experiences, taking me to Europe, U.K., Japan, and South Africa. However, without a doubt, the highlight of my quilting career was working with C&T to publish my book, *Beyond the Horizon.* It was a truly positive and wonderful experience. I learned so much, and the process of publishing helped me grow as an artist.

FAVORITE QUILTING EXPERIENCE

I think the essence of why women have flocked to quilting in droves is that quilting is the ancient process of stitching cloth that gives solace and meaning—we can talk about our lives, telling our stories through the fabric medium, no matter what degree of skill we have.

Quilting rules seem to respond so well to being broken that many of us feel comfortable without too many rules as we approach the quilt as an art form for self-expression.

SIGNIFICANT CHANGES IN THE LAST 20 YEARS

I think the computer is revolutionizing quilting, both in how quilts are made, and how our community interacts. The computer is a tool to download software for sewing machines, manipulate images and print them out on fabric on our printers, design quilts, order fabric or books from anywhere in the world, or take a workshop. In many ways, the computer is able to provide us with highly specialized and technical information more immediately than magazines can.

The computer's impact on the worldwide community of quilters is profound and enriching. As I sit in rather remote Newfoundland, I am connected daily with quilters around the world. Just today, I received emails from quilters in the Arctic, Abu Dhabi, and Japan. I participate in Web groups that have a thousand quilters sharing ideas. The latest news flash in the quilting world is instantly spun around the world. I can visit quilters' studios and see work they've just finished, view exhibitions, and discover the top prizewinner in a show the same day it's awarded! It's exciting communication and is building community in a powerful and immediate way.

1994

Paula Nadelstern

FAVORITE QUILTING STORY

It's a beautiful fall morning and I'm racing up the New York Thruway with two sleeping high school seniors in the backseat and the mom of the one who's not mine riding shotgun. The two seniors, Ariel, my daughter, and Nick, live in the same apartment building, have been friends since they were a few weeks old, and have gone to school together every step of the way . . . so far. Now they both have late morning college interview appointments.

As we get closer to our exit, we wake the kids up, partly to feed them and partly to prep them. I earnestly try to explain the fine points of being an interviewee, how this is their chance to shape a view that makes them unique, how the goal is not to fit into the crowd but to rise above it, how they have to advocate for themselves. Through the rearview mirror, I can see them rolling their eyes and smirking as I suggest that Nick might talk about the elaborate architectural structures he creates on the computer and Ariel could mention that she's familiar with traditional and contemporary quiltmaking. "Those aren't my interests," Ariel quickly responded. "I'm not a quilter."

You know the drill, after we obediently march through the impressive campus herded by mature upperclassmen, it's time for Ariel's interview. I'm waiting with the other parents when she bounces out, all excited. "Guess what, Mom!" Ariel exclaims, introducing me to the interviewer trailing close behind her, "She's a quilter!"

Favorite QUILTING TIP

I'M ON A CONSTANT QUEST FOR THE PERFECT WAY TO MARK TEMPLATES ON DARK-COLORED FABRIC. IN THIS CASE, PERFECT MEANS A THIN, VISIBLE LINE THAT (1) STAYS THIN AND VISIBLE AND (2) GLIDES SMOOTHLY WITHOUT STRETCHING THE FABRIC.

I AM TAKING A DEEP BREATH, ADMITTING I'M NOT A PURIST, AND PUTTING THIS OUT THERE: CONSIDER THE MERITS OF THOSE NEWFANGLED, LIGHT-COLORED, PERMANENT, AND ACID-FREE IMPLEMENTS CALLED GELL INK PENS. USE THEM TO MARK CUTTING LINES, NOT SEWING LINES. PICK A PRETTY PASTEL TO TRACE AROUND THE EDGE OF A TEMPLATE. IT DOESN'T BLEED, AND SINCE YOU CUT FABRIC PATCHES THE SAME WAY YOU DO TEMPLATES—BY AIMING STRAIGHT DOWN THE MIDDLE OF THE MARKED LINE—MOST OF THE LINE DISAPPEARS ANYWAY. SO, IF THE FUTURE PRODUCES HINDSIGHT THAT REVEALS THE ERROR OF OUR WAYS, WE CAN STILL SLEEP EASY.

Elly Sienkiewicz

Elly Sienkiewicz

Ruth B. McDowell

Susanna Oroyan

1994

Hari Walner

FAVORITE QUILTING STORIES

When I was working on *Exploring Machine Trapunto*, C&T needed to design the cover. To be expedient, I made and sent only a small, quilted portion of the quilt I had designed. When it was time to make the complete quilt, I discovered that I only had a few scraps of the fabric left. I sent tiny little scraps all over the country; no luck, no one had any left. I showed a scrap of that fabric to students in a class I was teaching in Nebraska and hung a 3" square of the fabric in our booth at the convention. When we returned home, there was a total of fifteen yards of that fabric from nine generous quilters. I was never so happy to pay for fabric in my life. Thank you, Nebraska quilters.

In 1987, I applied for a job as an illustrator with *Quilter's Newsletter Magazine*. Although I had extensive illustration experience, I had never quilted. When the founder/publisher-in-chief, Bonnie Leman, asked me if I could make a quilt, I asked her if she could give me a week. She agreed. I left her office and immediately looked in the yellow pages under "Q." I bought a rotary cutter, a little mat, a book, and some fabric. I found the sewing machine in the basement, read about $1/4$" seam allowances, cut the fabric, and sewed. Miraculously, I finished the top that week. Later, I discovered how to baste and hand quilt. I think my quilting stitches on this quilt are about three stitches to the inch. Well, maybe not *quite* that small.

First Quilt

Recent Quilt

Quilt San Diego

Elly Sienkiewicz

Alex Anderson

Yvonne Porcella

1994

Wendy Hill

FAVORITE QUILTING STORY

Never underestimate the power of a quilt! Quilts I made for baby nieces and nephews were still being used by teenagers and are still treasured by these same young adults today. My mother with Alzheimer's couldn't remember being married for 60 years or what she'd said or done five minutes earlier, but she remembered I was making her a kitty-cat wallhanging. Whether made to cuddle under or to look at, quilts have the power to touch our hearts and minds.

SIGNIFICANT CHANGES IN THE LAST 20 YEARS

The acceptance of machine quilting and the exploration and exploitation of thread texturing have been major changes in the past decade.

FAVORITE QUILTING QUOTES

You already have what you need to begin.

". . . you don't need much to make a quilt; just desire, an idea, and fabric."
Joan Colvin.

Favorite QUILTING TIP

I often collect dozens of pieces of fabric ½ yard or smaller for a project. When prewashing, these small pieces twist around each other and the washing machine agitator. Now, I sort the fabrics into color piles, with "like" colors in each pile. Then I zigzag the fabrics together (overlapping the fabric edges a bit) to make longer lengths of up to three yards. The big pieces wash beautifully. Dry until just barely damp, then cut apart and iron (or allow to air dry over the ironing board). I now use one of the dye magnet sheets that collect free dye in the wash water, and I haven't had a problem with color migration since.

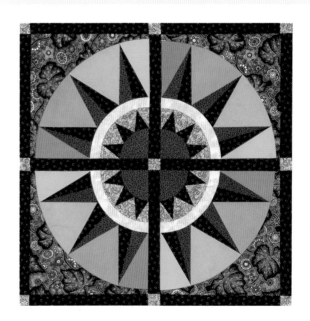

Virginia Avery

1994

Virginia Avery

1994

Judith Baker Montano

1995

Elly Sienkiewicz

1995

Jean Wells

1995

Helen Kelley

FAVORITE QUILTING EXPERIENCE

There is no more joyful way to celebrate than to make a quilt. My first quilt was made in anticipation of my wedding. Since that time every exciting event has been celebrated with a quilt—my daughters' marriages, the births of grandchildren, grandchildren's weddings, and the births of their children. I have stitched holiday excursions and solemn occasions into quilts. Once I made a quilt simply to celebrate the glorious monarch butterfly that lit in the middle of my flaming marigolds. The aspect of a celebration sends my mind into a frenzy of color and texture and pattern. The wonder of it is there are so many people in this world that react in exactly the same way as I do. The act of making a quilt is itself a celebration.

▩ Favorite QUILTING TIP

COLORS FOR YOUR QUILT THAT MATCH EXACTLY, MOVING RIGHT DOWN THE LINE IN HUE AND TONE, WILL PRODUCE A QUILT THAT WILL BE CALM AND SEDATE. TO ADD EXCITEMENT TO YOUR QUILT, LET YOUR COLORS CLASH A BIT. LEMONADE TINGLES AND SPARKLES ON THE TONGUE. IN THE SAME WAY, COLORS THAT DON'T QUITE MATCH WILL TINGLE AND SPARKLE ON THE EYE.

Pat Campbell

SIGNIFICANT CHANGES IN THE LAST 20 YEARS

The quiltmakers palette has changed drastically. Bold, glorious color now stands out to me as the most significant change in the most recent years. My first Jacobean-style quilt was worked on a black background with neon colors. Quiltmakers often tell me that it opened the door for them to explore the use of vivid colors and introduced the quilt world to fantasy botanicals.

Harriet Hargrave

Joen Wolfrom

Jinny Beyer

Helen Kelley

1995

Margaret Miller

FAVORITE QUILTING STORY

Long ago, I gave up quilting in airports, or engaging in conversations on airplanes about my livelihood, because I didn't want yet one more palm-pilot toting businessman with a cordless phone to his ear tell me his "aunt used to crochet, too!" (And that's a quote!)

My favorite story of my career being misunderstood happened in the middle of the night as I boarded a shuttle bus to the airport, en route to New Zealand for three weeks of teaching quilt-making. I was really tired, and was praying that I wouldn't get a "chatty" van driver. I managed to climb aboard, and when the driver energetically popped onto his seat, his cheery greeting was "AND where are you going today?"

"New Zealand," I answered shortly.

"For business or pleasure?" continued the chirpy voice from behind the steering wheel.

"Business," said I.

"Well, what do you do for a living?" replied the undaunted conversationalist.

"I teach quiltmaking all over the world," was my curt reply. That response slowed him down a bit—but he finally said, "They PAY YOU to do THAT?!"

End of conversation . . .

FAVORITE QUILTING QUOTE

. . . WHICH I BELIEVE IN, AND USE OFTEN:

NEVER USE TWO FABRICS WHEN YOU CAN USE TWENTY!

Favorite QUILTING TIP

WHEN JOINING TWO PIECES OF GRAPH PAPER TOGETHER IN ORDER TO DRAFT LARGE TEMPLATES, FIRST CUT OFF TWO ADJACENT CORNERS OF ONE PIECE, AND OVERLAP IT ONTO THE OTHER PIECE OF GRAPH PAPER. WITH THE CORNERS CUT OFF, YOU CAN SEE THE HORIZONTAL AND VERTICAL GRAPH PAPER LINES ON BOTH SHEETS OF PAPER, FOR QUICKER AND MORE ACCURATE JOINING.

Judy Mathieson

Roberta Horton

Chalotte Patera

Charlotte Warr Andersen

1995

Judy B. Dales

FAVORITE SEWING STORY

When I was young, I was a very impatient sewer. I had no patience for any of the pitfalls of dressmaking. I hated ripping out seams. A poorly behaved sewing machine put me into a rage, and running out of bobbin thread would frustrate me no end! I took no pride in the various steps required to produce a well-made garment, but was always anxious and hurrying to get to the finished product.

When I was in eighth grade, I was a member of our local 4-H club and we were learning to sew. Rather than choose a simple project that I could do well, I had my heart set on something fancy.

My grandmother and 4-H leader both tried to dissuade me from this particular pattern, but I was determined. Of course, it was a disaster from start to finish. I ripped and sewed, ripped and sewed until every seam was in shreds. When the project was finally finished, I modeled it in the 4-H fashion show.

Unfortunately, I don't think I learned nearly enough from this experience, but it was a beginning. And over the years, it has become a benchmark—something against which to measure progress. For eventually I discovered quiltmaking, and it was through making quilts that I learned to do things slowly and carefully the first time. I learned that if a seam wasn't done right, it was better to rip it out, because it was not going to correct itself as the work progressed. I have gained patience and I don't have to rush to the finished product, because I now enjoy the process and take pleasure in doing each step properly. I truly understand the old saying that if something is worth doing, it is worth doing well.

FAVORITE QUILTING QUOTE

IF IT'S NOT FUN, WHY ARE WE DOING IT?

THIS STATEMENT SUMS UP MY FEELINGS ABOUT QUILTMAKING. LIFE IS TOO SHORT TO SPEND YOUR TIME DOING THINGS YOU DON'T LIKE, SO BE SURE YOUR QUILTMAKING IS FUN. WORK WITH TEACHERS WHO MAKE LEARNING A JOY, CHOOSE TECHNIQUES THAT APPEAL TO YOU, WORK WITH COLORS THAT MAKE YOUR HEART SING, APPROACH EACH TASK WITH ENTHUSIASM AND DETERMINATION, AND ENJOY THE SENSE OF SATISFACTION WHEN A TASK IS COMPLETED. THAT, TO ME, IS FUN!

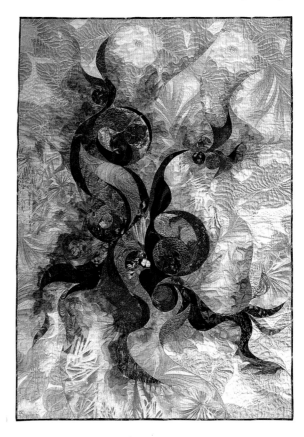

Valerie Hearder

Gai Perry

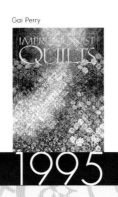

Nancy Crow

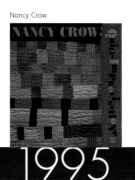

Blanche Young & Darlene Young Stone

1995   1995   1995   1996

Judy Heim

FAVORITE QUILTING STORY

My mother tossed out a ragged quilt she had been given as a wedding gift 40 years before. I threw it on my bed because I remembered sleeping under it as a kid. Time passed and it grew more ragged.

Eventually I found myself piecing it back together, whipstitching frayed patches cut from flour sack dresses beside ones cut from men's striped Sunday-good pants. I discovered that the back of the quilt was cobbled together from cornmeal sacks and burlap from chicken-feed bags. The women dyed them yellow with skins from onions they had grown themselves. They hand stitched everything with thread they sent their children to unravel from feed sacks. As they worked they chewed tobacco, they kept watch on their kids from the wooden porch where they sat looking out over the cotton fields. They gave a quilt like this to every "kin" upon their marriage.

When I finally saw a picture of the women who made my quilt I gasped to my mother, "Boy, they look scary!"

She laughed and said, "They were a feisty bunch." In the tattered black-and-white photo my grandmothers stand shoulder-to-shoulder with their mothers and aunts, their arms crossed, their faces fierce. They look nearly indomitable in their long calico dresses whose dour, modest prints I recognize as having been sacrificed for patches in my quilts. Their large black boots look capable of carrying them at earnest speed across any unwilling terrain.

I find comfort in the fact that each time I walk into the living room I see the quilt draped over my couch patched by such tough-spirited women. It almost hovers in the room like a souvenir of all the sacrifices that have been made for my parents and me to enjoy an easy, happy life. When I find myself grousing over the inanities of modern life, the quilt stops me cold. I almost hang my head in shame. These women suffered, lived hard, gave everything they had. What is my excuse for not doing likewise?

I'm still not a good quilter. My stitches are crooked, my quilt tops never lie flat. But every time I pick up a needle I remind myself that if a group of women in calico dresses on a mountaintop can tame a land and a country, as well as raise families and even find time to quilt, there is little that the human spirit cannot achieve.

Roberta Horton

Hari Walner

Jean & Valori Wells

Candace Kling

Mary Mashuta

1996

Gloria Hansen

SIGNIFICANT CHANGES IN THE LAST 20 YEARS

I took my first formal quilting class in 1981. Since that time, for me there are two significant developments that enhance my quiltmaking; the personal computer and the Internet. After purchasing my first Macintosh, I immediately became hooked on using the computer as a design tool. Additionally, my inkjet printers allow me to print digital images and abstract designs onto fabric. This, in combination with my painted and dyed fabrics, provides me with an exciting, personalized palette.

Connection to the Internet has introduced me to quilters all over the world. Through my online friendships, I continue to have many quilting opportunities that I may not otherwise have had, including writing the *Free Stuff* series for C&T. I also am inspired on a regular basis to stretch my quilting boundaries. I encourage all quilters to connect to the Internet. Opportunities, myriads of information, and plenty of galleries and other visual treats are waiting to be discovered.

PROUDEST C&T EXPERIENCE

Being associated with such a class act!

Favorite QUILTING TIP

I KEEP A RECORD OF MY QUILTS. THE MAIN PAGE OF EACH QUILT INCLUDES THE QUILT TITLE, DATE COMPLETED, DIMENSIONS, A SMALL DESCRIPTION, AND FULL-VIEW AND CLOSE-UP PHOTOS. ADDITIONAL CLEAR PLASTIC PAGES INCLUDE FABRIC MOCK-UPS, SCRAPS OF FABRIC SEWN ONTO A SHEET OF PAPER, SKETCHES, DESIGN VARIATIONS, AND OTHER NOTES THAT I STORE IN THREE-RING BINDERS. PERIODICALLY, I HAVE COLOR PHOTOCOPIES MADE OF ALL THE MAIN PAGES, WHICH I KEEP IN SEPARATE PRESENTATION BOOKS. I BRING THESE PRESENTATION BOOKS, RATHER THAN THE ORIGINALS, WITH ME WHEN I AM TEACHING.

Sally Collins

Cheryl Greider Bradkin

Diana Leone

Quilt San Diego

Patty McCormick

1996

Girls Incorporated

PROUDEST C&T EXPERIENCE

Planning for Girls Inc.'s *Women of Taste* quilt exhibit, sponsored by the Smithsonian Institution's Traveling Exhibition Service, was barely underway when it seemed obvious that a book capturing the stories of the collaborations between quilters and chefs should be written and published.

We ventured into this new arena with few preconceptions, lots of energy, and a readiness to learn a new field. Our first meeting with Todd went exceptionally well and in our minds we were ready to forge ahead. While Todd worked internally making decisions, we waited, semi-patiently, to hear whether this was a viable match. Unequivocally, the two letters, one from C&T and one from the Smithsonian both stating their interest and eagerness to go forward with the project, are sources of immense pride.

The finished product is far beyond our greatest expectations—it is a beautifully designed and executed book that everyday reminds us of Girls Inc.'s mission to be *strong, smart, and bold*.
— LYNN RICHARDS

Rebecca Wat

FAVORITE QUILTING EXPERIENCE

When I was quilting for my then three-year-old boy, he was very excited about it, paying attention to every move I made even though it was just an ordinary quilt.

GREATEST QUILTING HURDLE

Quilting under time pressure.

SIGNIFICANT CHANGES IN THE LAST 20 YEARS

The emergence of art quilts, and the increasing popularity of quilting in foreign countries have shown amazing changes.

Ruth B. McDowell

Alex Anderson

Katie Pasquini Masopust

Diane Leone

Paula Nadelstern

1996

Sharyn Craig

FAVORITE QUILTING QUOTE

IT IS OKAY TO FAIL, BUT IT IS NOT OKAY *NOT* TO TRY FOR FEAR OF FAILURE.

I use these words over and over again in my lectures and workshops. It is a phrase I came up with years ago, that has just "stuck." I feel we learn best through our trials and efforts. These attempts do not always lead to success, but unless we are willing to take that chance we will never know whether we can achieve the goal. The simple fact that we were willing to attempt and try something new and different is what counts.

GREATEST QUILTING HURDLE

Undoubtedly it was the co-authoring of *The Art of Classic Quiltmaking* with Harriet Hargrave. When you take two very strong-willed, opinionated people and team them up to write an encyclopedia guidebook on quiltmaking, you are looking at a huge challenge. Harriet and I had been friends for years before this opportunity presented itself. When Harriet asked me to do this with her I was overwhelmed with the scope of the project. My biggest concern was if we could maintain our friendship throughout the writing of the book. The friendship was far more important than any book. So, we set up some guidelines for the project. Number one was that we agreed to disagree. We also agreed that we would be writing a guidebook and not a rulebook. We next agreed to talk about anything that disturbed either of us at the time it happened, rather than allow anything to fester.

It was not an easy decision, but the final deciding factor for me was my own words, "It is okay to fail. But it is not okay *not* to try for fear of failure."

The book was a huge project. It was a three-year commitment on each of our parts from the day we shook hands on the project, until the book was in our hands. It was an incredible learning experience for both of us. And best of all, we are still great friends!

Diana McClun & Laura Nownes

Celia Y. Oliver

Jean Wells

Joen Wolfrom

Barbara Brackman

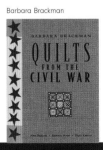

1997

Diane Phalen

PROUDEST C&T EXPERIENCE

My proudest accomplishment was my book, *Diane Phalen Quilts*. To have quilters create quilts from within my paintings was an absolute thrill. I have always felt that quilting was an art form in fabric. The same elements that are in painting are present in quiltmaking, including considerations of effect, color scheme, design style, and color balance. Seasons always have a special effect on my work; I paint with the seasons. I love the spring and summer flowers. When the air starts turning cooler and brisker, I sense the autumn and start painting with the mood of that favorite season. Each season has its special colors and smells.

FAVORITE QUILTING EXPERIENCE

Working with all of the great quilt artists who created the quilts that went along with the paintings was wonderful. They put their own special touch into each quilt.

SIGNIFICANT CHANGES IN THE LAST 20 YEARS

The quilts created 20 years ago were mostly based on traditional patterns and traditional piecing. Each year I notice fewer traditional patterns and more contemporary patterns emerging. The past few years I have been overwhelmed with all of the "paintings" created by fabric. The quilts are a canvas of color and perspective, so lifelike that from afar you would think you were looking at a painting. Up close, you can see all the thousands of pieces of fabric and multicolored threads—plain, metallic, and luminescent. Fabrics are brighter, bolder, and more textured. I am still the biggest fan of traditional patterns, especially the Amish patterns. I am always amazed at the beauty of the plain black background and traditional Amish colors that are so radiant.

One thing that hasn't changed in quilting is the generosity, happiness, and friendliness of the quilters themselves. I am always overwhelmed at their love of their craft. And now I have created my first quilt block (page 109). My sewing skills have a lot to be desired as there was a lot of tangling of thread and needle-stabbing in this project . . . but it was fun, too, and that is what life is all about.

Susanna Oroyan

Harriet Hargrave

Gai Perry

Wendy Hill

1997

The Jim Henson Company/Sesame Workshop

FAVORITE QUILTING STORY

When I began working for the Muppet Workshop as a stitcher in 1982, I soon realized I had landed in a wonderful place full of very talented and very funny people. One Christmas, I used the big tables at the workshop after hours to cut and sew my first quilt as a gift for my parents. When I look at that quilt now, it was really a beginner's effort; few corners met neatly and it was tied instead of quilted. But it was an expression of love for my mother and father, and their delight was very encouraging to me. A further encouragement was being asked to make Kermit puppets for the film production, *The Muppets Take Manhattan*. I had to make quite a few trial heads until one was good enough to be used for Kermit, and my minimal sewing skills were strengthened with that work.

In the late 1980s, Stephen Rotondaro unknowingly started a tradition when he organized a baby quilt for a co-worker. This one quilt led to many others, and there are now nearly 40 quilts made by people who have worked at the Muppets. I received a quilt of my own when my son was born in 1991.

In 1999, after seeing a magazine article on these quilts, C&T contacted The Jim Henson Company to do a book on them, including patterns based on some of the designs we had created. Working with the patient editor Barb Kuhn, who understood the very personal nature of each quilt, was a great pleasure. The resulting book was a great tribute to the incredible people who worked together under Jim Henson and all their fantastic creativity and silliness.

SIGNIFICANT CHANGES IN THE LAST 20 YEARS

Many things have changed at the Muppets over the last years: Jim Henson died in 1990, and Richard Hunt, puppeteer of Beaker and Scooter and other characters, died of AIDS a few years later. The book embodies the beauty and creativity that came together as a result of working with wonderfully talented people.

— LAUREN ATTINELLO

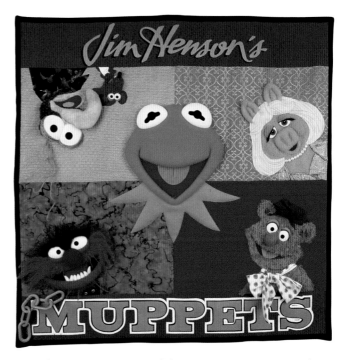

Kermit the Frog™ appears courtesy of The Jim Henson Company. © 2002 The Jim Henson Company. JIM HENSON'S mark & logo, MUPPETS mark & logo, MUPPET, KERMIT THE FROG character and elements are trademarks of The Jim Henson Company. All Rights Reserved.

Judith Baker Montano

Jean Ray Laury

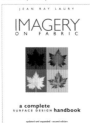

Yvonne Porcella

Alex Anderson

1997

Jane A. Sassaman

PROUDEST C&T EXPERIENCE

The Quilted Garden is the materialization of a dream, thanks to C&T. It is wonderful to have 20 years of work compiled in one volume, and to encourage other quilters and designers to use their personal circumstances to their best advantage.

The Quilted Garden has uncovered the world for this quiet quilter. As a teacher, I have been invited to exotic locations around the globe. I've seen Chocolate Lilies in the Yukon, bathed outdoors on a landscaped hillside in Japan, and photographed Monkey Puzzle trees in New Zealand. But best of all are the wonderful new friends I've met on the road and in correspondence. I am lucky to have such thoughtful and talented colleagues.

So, thank you C&T for your investment of time on my behalf. And I wish you another 20 years of success.

Nancy Johnson-Srebro

Favorite QUILTING TIP

MACHINE PIECE WITH AN OPEN-TOE WALKING FOOT. THIS FOOT WILL NOT TWIST OR PULL THE FABRIC.

FAVORITE QUILTING STORY

Grandma Carrison was my mentor while I made my first quilt. She asked me to cut a 6" square template from paper and pin it on my fabric. Using regular (dull) scissors, I cut around the template. After cutting about two dozen squares, I noticed some of the squares were not the same size. I called Gram and said, "My blocks don't seem to be the same size."

She replied, "Are you cutting any of the paper template off when you cut around it?"

I replied, "No! Well, only once in a while. . ." That was my first lesson in accuracy, and it has stuck with me all these years.

PROUDEST C&T QUILTING EXPERIENCE

I was lecturing in Hilton Head Island, South Carolina, and a woman I didn't know stood up and thanked me for passing quilting on to the next generation. She said that she and her granddaughter were going to make some of the blocks from my *Block Magic* book. I get goose bumps every time I think about the impact my books will have on future generations.

Alex Anderson

Michael James

Deidre Scherer

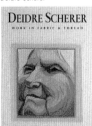

Ruth B. McDowell

1998

Jan Mullen

PROUDEST C&T EXPERIENCE

I'm very proud I have made it easier for many quilters to relax and use fabric and color more effectively. For them, my methods have been integral in putting the fun back into their quilting. I see them relaxing with the construction and then becoming more and more confident about fabric selections. For others, permission to break rules they have been so well taught has, in turn, given them permission to make their own decisions.

Favorite QUILTING TIPS

GET TO KNOW YOUR FABRIC. CATALOG IT IN YOUR HEAD AS WELL AS ON YOUR SHELVES; WHILE YOU WASH AND IRON IT, AS YOU PUT IT IN ITS SELECT POSITION IN YOUR COLLECTION, AND LATER WHEN YOU ARE SEARCHING FOR PROJECT FABRIC.

GET THE COLORS TO FIGHT! VISUAL SPARRING INSPIRES US ALL. THIS CAN BE DONE WITH ANY PALETTE—BRIGHTS, COUNTRY, OR PASTELS. IT'S A MATTER OF HOW FAR TO TAKE THE FIGHT—YOU ARE THE REFEREE; LET YOUR EYES BE THE JUDGE.

AUDITION FABRIC FOR DIFFERENT ROLES—MAJOR, SUPPORT, OR BIT PLAYER. ALL ARE ESSENTIAL IN MAKING YOUR QUILT A SHOWSTOPPER.

FAVORITE QUILTING QUOTE

JAN'S WICKED SO YOU CAN BE . . . AND THE QUILT POLICE WON'T GET YOU!

Louisa Smith

FAVORITE QUILTING QUOTE

REMEMBER, EVERY MISTAKE IS A VALUABLE LESSON LEARNED, AND BRINGS YOU ONE STEP CLOSER TO PERFECTION.

SIGNIFICANT CHANGES IN THE LAST 20 YEARS

The availability of many incredible quilting tools makes quilt-making today much easier, much faster, and also more precise! And let's not forget today's new sewing machines with the most incredible features, such as perfect $1/4"$ seam allowances, machine quilting, and embroidery units, just to name a few.

Favorite QUILTING TIP

TO MAKE VERY LARGE CIRCLES, SEMI-CIRCLES, OR QUARTER-CIRCLES, MAKE A LARGE COMPASS BY DRILLING HOLES 1" APART ALONG THE ENTIRE LENGTH OF A YARDSTICK. USE A PUSHPIN TO ANCHOR, AND A PENCIL IN THE APPROPRIATE HOLE TO MARK THE ARCS. THE SAME PROCEDURE COULD BE USED FOR SMALLER CIRCLES BY USING A PLASTIC DRAFTING RULER AND POKING HOLES WITH A PUSHPIN EVERY $1/2"$ OR SO.

Hari Walner

Elly Sienkiewicz

Margaret J. Miller

Amy Barickman

1998

Larraine Scouler

FAVORITE C&T EXPERIENCE

I live in Sydney, Australia, half a world away, possibly the absolute furthest anyone can physically be from the C&T office in Concord, California. Finally meeting the editorial, production, and marketing people when I visited the U.S. in 2001 was the icing on the cake of publishing for me; putting names and faces to voices and email messages finally made me feel a part of the C&T family.

I am proud of the reflected glory of being a C&T author. The deserved reputation of C&T as leader in the quilting publication industry has not happened accidentally. The high standards in both pre- and post-production, combined with the professionalism of the staff, justify this position, and I am honored to be a part of it.

SIGNIFICANT CHANGES IN THE LAST 20 YEARS

I look to the future and the Internet. This new medium of the millennium is creating new communities of quilters beyond the boundaries of time and distance; the contacts may be virtual but the connections are real. The television show *X-Files* put it best, "We are not alone."

 Favorite QUILTING TIP & QUOTE

"QUILT NOW, PERFECTION LATER." SAID BY WHOM AND WHERE IS UNKNOWN TO ME. BUT DOESN'T THIS SAY IT ALL, AS SO MANY QUILTERS PUT TOO MUCH PRESSURE ON THEMSELVES TO DO IT "RIGHT" THE FIRST TIME, OFTEN HESITATING TO TAKE ON NEW CHALLENGES FOR FEAR OF FAILURE!

GREATEST QUILTING HURDLE

My greatest quilting hurdle has always been myself. I've never doubted my technical skills, but like many of you, I've hesitated at the prospect of new challenges. I would only have regrets if I had *not* entered that first quilt show; or put my reputation on the line in that first shop as a teacher; or volunteered for a committee of the national quilting guild; or submitted my ideas to a publisher; or if I had taken the first no as the final answer. I am better for having done all these things and more, and I've come to realize that the worst thing would be not to have tried and lost . . . but not to have tried at all.

Yvonne Porcella

Carol Armstrong

Judy B. Dales

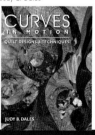

Roberta Horton

1998

Mary Lou Weidman

FAVORITE QUILTING QUOTE

EVERY EVENT IN LIFE IS A QUILT WAITING TO HAPPEN.

FAVORITE QUILTING STORY

When my children were home and going to school, I made a full-size quilt with five figures on the front holding hands, with the saying "The Best Things in Life Are Not Things." One day one of us was sick, and used the quilt to keep warm. From that day forward it was the "Sick Quilt." Each one of us over the years has used the Sick Quilt for comfort, warmth, and healing. It is our favorite quilt. Last year I was grocery shopping, and when I came home, my son Jason—who lives in his own home—was on the sofa with the Sick Quilt covering him. He glanced up and said, "Bad day at work." That was the best thing anyone had ever said to me about one of my quilts.

SIGNIFICANT CHANGES IN THE LAST 20 YEARS

Style does not seem to be as important as it once was. I started making story quilts in 1987, after quilting traditional quilts since 1974. At the time, I was going it alone and most quilters did not understand my quilts. Time has changed all of that, and I think it is a blessing that most quilters and quilt lovers can see that there is room for every type and style of quilt, whether traditional or contemporary. It is a blessing to share the love of quilting and the love of quilters as a common theme.

PROUDEST C&T EXPERIENCE

I once cut out articles and followed statements of famous quilters who wrote books for C&T. I had no idea that one day I would be lucky enough to be an author for C&T Publishing. With all of my accomplishments, I think this is one of my proudest, and one of the nicest surprises. In all honesty, I have to say everyone I worked with at C&T was the type of quilter and friend I wanted when I entered into quilting.

Ruth Reynolds

Patricia B. Campbell & Mimi Ayars

Charlotte Warr Andersen

Judy Heim & Gloria Hansen

Judith Baker Montano

1998

Marie-Christine Flocard

FAVORITE QUILTING STORY

On my way back from the U.S. to France I was seated at the back of the airplane cabin. Almost everybody was either asleep or watching the movie. Of course, I was quilting. Suddenly with the feeling of someone watching me, I raised my head. It was the female captain.

Hearing my accent, she said: "Oh! A French quilter! You know, I am a quilter too! Immediately, she took the empty seat and we started to talk about quilting in France.

What a chat; in the middle of the night some 30,000 feet above the Atlantic Ocean, there I was, talking patchwork with the head pilot of my aircraft. (Later my husband said it could only have been stranger if the captain had been a man!) She took the address of the shop I work at in Paris and returned to the cockpit. Two days later, as I was teaching at the shop, she came in. We talked again and she managed to buy a load of French fabrics as cargo for her return flight. Since then, each time I board a flight, I check to see who the captain is.

Cosabeth Parriaud

FAVORITE C&T EXPERIENCE

The week I spent with our editor Beate Nellemann, my co-author, and our photographer Jean-Michael André in June of 2001 in Provence for the photo shooting of our book, *Provence Quilts and Cuisine*. It was fabulous; we worked hard but in complete harmony, looking for the right places for taking the photos, cooking the recipes, and enjoying being in this wonderful part of France . . . an unforgettable experience!

Favorite QUILTING TIP

IT IS GOOD TO FOLLOW THE RULES FROM YOUR TEACHER OR FROM YOUR FIRST QUILTING BOOK WHEN YOU START QUILTING IN ORDER TO MASTER THE DIFFERENT TECHNIQUES. YOU MUST ALSO LEARN HOW TO BREAK THESE RULES TO DEVELOP YOUR OWN STYLE. THERE ARE NO ABSOLUTE RULES; FOLLOW YOUR INSTINCTS, TRUST YOUR FEELINGS AND YOURSELF.

Jean & Valori Wells
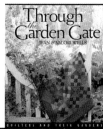

Judy Heim & Gloria Hansen

Judy Heim & Gloria Hansen

Judy Heim & Gloria Hansen

Judy Heim & Gloria Hansen

1999

Cyndy Rymer

FAVORITE C&T STORY

A few years ago, my husband was offered a job in the San Francisco Bay Area. We flew out there, were wined and dined, and then went house hunting. Sticker shock! We reluctantly agreed to go back and stay in Massachusetts. Upon my return to Hopkinton, I received a letter from Joyce Lytle, in California. I had contacted her for information about guilds in the Bay Area, and she was kind enough to write a nice long letter. She said she worked at C&T and that there were two editorial job openings IF I was interested. My jaw dropped. After doing freelance editorial work at home for years, I was looking for a way to re-enter the job market. I called Joyce and asked her to PLEASE hold the part-time job for me. Then, I called my husband and told him to accept the job that had been offered to him. A month later we moved to California, and it's been great!

SIGNIFICANT CHANGES IN THE LAST 20 YEARS

Absolutely, the biggest change has been the rotary cutter. The number of quilt retreats has also dramatically increased; they are my favorite vacations.

Jennifer Rounds

FAVORITE QUILTING QUOTE

THIS ONE IS MINE—WHENEVER I DESIGN A SCRAPPY QUILT I CHANT THIS MANTRA: RANDOM ACTS OF RANDOMNESS. OKAY, IT'S WEIRD, BUT IT HELPS ME DISTRIBUTE COLOR AND PATTERN ACROSS THE SURFACE OF A QUILT.

IF ALL ELSE FAILS, USE A BLACK AND WHITE FABRIC TO JAZZ THINGS UP.

Favorite QUILTING TIP

I GOT THIS FROM ALEX ANDERSON, WHO SAID SHE PICKED IT UP FROM JEAN WELLS—BEYOND THAT, I HAVEN'T A CLUE. KEEP A TINY FABRIC SCRAP HANDY WHENEVER YOU ARE PIECING, AND FEED THE SCRAP INTO THE SEWING MACHINE TO START SEWING. USE THE SCRAP TO BEGIN AND END ANY SEWING SEQUENCE AND AVOID THREAD BALLS COLLECTING ON THE UNDERSIDE OF YOUR SEWING. IT'S A GREAT WAY TO KEEP AN EVEN FLOW AND ELIMINATES THE NEED TO HOLD THE TOP AND BOBBIN THREADS AS YOU PRESS THE FOOT PEDAL.

Freddy Moran

Alex Anderson

Jennifer Gilbert
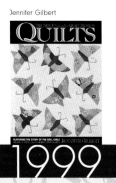

Joen Wolfrom
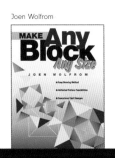

Susanna Oroyan

1999

Dilys A. Fronks

FAVORITE QUILTING QUOTE

NOT UNTIL MY INTRODUCTION TO QUILTMAKING IN 1984, DID I REALIZE THAT I POSSESSED A CREATIVE BONE IN MY BODY, A FEEL FOR COLOR, OR AN APTITUDE FOR DESIGN. I ATTENDED A ONE-DAY WORKSHOP ON APPLIQUÉ AND AS I WORKED ON THAT FIRST PILLOW FRONT, I KNEW INSTINCTIVELY WHERE I WANTED TO BE, WITHOUT REALIZING I HAD BEEN SEARCHING FOR SOMEWHERE TO GO. MY FIRST QUILT OPENED THE DOORS TO THIS AWARENESS. NOW, MY FAVORITE EXPRESSION IS "I FEEL A QUILT COMING ON!" I JUST CAN'T HELP MYSELF.

FAVORITE QUILTING EXPERIENCE

I have often pondered on how similar the word "quilt" is to the word "guilt." And yet, whilst quilting, how often have I felt guilty about not preparing this meal, or cleaning that cupboard because, let's face it, I'd rather be quilting—spending time in my workshop on what I so enjoy! Initially, I used to shoulder the mantle of guilt willingly as I strove to be superhuman in the management of home, family, and the business of quiltmaking. And then, oh joy, I was lucky enough to get a man's eye view of it all!

I won a major championship with an entry in a U.K. show in 1986, and my greatest delight was to lurk around this quilt to witness the spontaneous reactions to it. Seeing a couple of gentlemen approaching, I watched them settle into a deep discussion in front of it. I leaned closer to catch perhaps a complimentary comment on color or an assessment of the subtle design qualities. Imagine how I laughed when I heard these words of wisdom, "Eeeeh, some lucky bugger's had hours of peace whilst she's been working on that one!" So, any future feelings of "guilt-while-u-quilt" vanished forever. Now my sewing is considered a peace-giving initiative!

Girls Incorporated

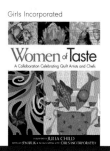

Mickey Lawler

Cozy Baker

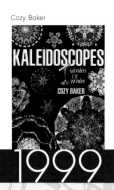

Jean Ray Laury

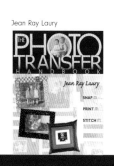

Gai Perry

1999

Trice Boerens

Favorite QUILTING TIP

USE THE WRONG SIDE OF A COTTON PRINT FABRIC WHEN YOU NEED A DIFFERENCE IN VALUE.

FAVORITE QUILTING STORY

In an effort to keep sharp scissors in the house, I buy a new pair and then hide them so well that I can't find them. One day last year I found a brand new pair in the vegetable crisper in the refrigerator.

Kathy Sandbach

PROUDEST C&T EXPERIENCE

A lifelong dream of publishing a book came true with the publication of *Show Me How to Machine Quilt.*

SIGNIFICANT CHANGES IN THE LAST 20 YEARS

Machine quilting is not only acceptable, but is now allowed to be an integral part of the quilt. Hallelujah!

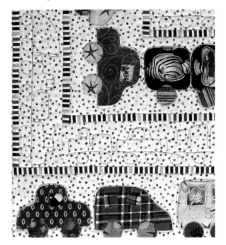

Nancy Odom

Favorite QUILTING TIP

MAKE A HANDLE FOR EVERY RULER YOU OWN, FOR JUST PENNIES!

1. CUT A 6" LENGTH OF 2"-WIDE, CLEAR HEAVY-DUTY PACKING TAPE.

2. FOLD THE TAPE IN HALF (STICKY SIDES TOGETHER), EXCEPT FOR THE LAST $1\frac{1}{2}$" AT EACH END.

3. PRESS THE ENDS OF TAPE TO THE CENTER OF THE RULER.

YOU CAN SEE THROUGH THIS TAPE HANDLE, IT FOLDS FLAT FOR STORAGE OR TRAVEL, AND IT NEVER GETS LOST!

Patrick Lose

Doreen Speckmann

Elly Sienkiewicz

Pepper Cory

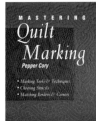

1999

Kristina Becker

PROUDEST C&T EXPERIENCE

I wrote a book about quilts my own way and they all listened.

FAVORITE QUILTING STORY

Several friends comment on my quilts, "You put a lot of yourself into these quilts!" They love the stories.

IN MEMORIAM:

C&T Publishing and the entire quilting community were saddened by the news that Kristina Becker, quilt artist and C&T author, passed away on November 28, 2002.

Kristina was a self-taught folk artist, dollmaker, and quilter who believed that the best art came from within the artist. Her goal was to inspire quilters and artists everywhere to create something all their own and to have fun with their art.

"The longer I live, the more I realize what a blessing it's been not to have attended art school or received formal training in textiles," Kristina said in her recently published book, *Come Listen to My Quilts*. "I've had a wonderful time throughout my life trying out new skills in needlework, and the process has always seemed new and exciting. Now I'm only bored when I don't have some needlework in my hands."

From 1980 to 1988, Kristina co-owned Going to Pieces, a thriving quilt shop in Pleasanton, California, and she was a founding member of the Amador Valley Quilters. She was always a favorite among colleagues and students, known for her warm, spirited personality and whimsical quilting style. Her one-of-a-kind appliqué quilts have received many awards and have been exhibited nationwide.

Kristina was very proud when her book, *Come Listen to My Quilts*, was published by C&T in Spring 2002.

"Kristina was a valued C&T author," says Amy Marson, publisher of C&T Publishing. "She brought her own sense of fun and inspiration to a wider audience by putting it together in book form, and we're grateful to have had the opportunity to publish her work."

Rebecca Wat

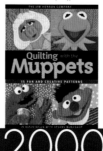

Harriet Hargrave & Sharyn Craig

Jim Henson Company/Sesame Workshop

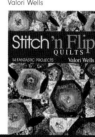

Gül Laporte

Valori Wells

2000

Lawry Thorn

SIGNIFICANT CHANGES IN THE LAST 20 YEARS

. . . the acceptance of machine quilting and the way it has changed with designs, threads, and machines. This is just another indication that it's all right to do your own thing in quilting, since we know there is no quilt jail!

 Favorite QUILTING TIPS

WHEN MACHINE QUILTING, LOOK JUST AHEAD OF THE NEEDLE—REMEMBER, NO NEED TO WATCH THE NEEDLE ITSELF, IT IS GOING TO GO UP AND DOWN AS LONG AS YOU HAVE YOUR FOOT ON THE PEDAL. THIS WAY, YOU WILL FOLLOW YOUR DESIGN VERY WELL.

WHEN PINNING A SEAM YOU WANT TO COME TOGETHER, STICK A PIN DIRECTLY THROUGH THE POINTS OF INTERSECTION, THEN PIN THE OTHER TWO PINS THROUGH THE FABRIC CLOSE BY, REMOVE THE PIN STICKING STRAIGHT THROUGH THE POINTS, AND SEW.

WHEN SEWING POINTS, HAVE THE NEEDLE GO THROUGH NOT THE POINT THAT THE THREADS CROSS EACH OTHER, BUT JUST TO THE SEAM SIDE OF THIS. WHEN PRESSING AND TURNING, THE POINT WILL COME OUT JUST RIGHT!

PROUDEST C&T EXPERIENCE

. . . is the fact that I have worked for and with Jean Wells in a variety of roles for over 20 years. We are able to keep coming up with new and different ideas to keep quilting fresh and moving ahead. She has been and is a great friend, resource, strength, encourager, and inspiration. Little did I know when I offered to fill in at the Stitchin' Post that it would lead to what it has, and give me so many opportunities in the world of quilting—meeting people, going places, and taking part in lectures and classes from so many great quilters.

Teaching quilting to so many, both beginners and accomplished quilters, is another accomplishment on my part that I am happy I am able to do.

Alex Anderson

Elly Sienkiewicz

Carol Armstrong

Margaret J. Miller

Susan Delaney-Mech, M.D.

2000

Linda Taylor

SIGNIFICANT CHANGES IN THE LAST 20 YEARS

I believe the most significant change in quilting in the last 20 years has been the innovative machine quilting. This has occurred for several reasons. First, our generation lives at a faster pace and desires completed projects. Second, we now have more tools available at our disposal to help us be more creative. We love the new technology, new machines, and variety of materials and information. It has created a whole new subculture within our society. It is a safe place to go in a world no longer as safe as we would like it to be.

And within the subculture of quilters is another subculture of longarm quilters, who, for the most part, finish other people's projects. And while they are working on these projects, they are creating their own art and developing and refining their skills, taking quilting into a new realm.

FAVORITE QUILTING QUOTE

THE PURSUIT OF EXCELLENCE IS GRATIFYING AND HEALTHY. THE PURSUIT OF PERFECTION IS FRUSTRATING, NEUROTIC, AND A TERRIBLE WASTE OF TIME.

GREATEST QUILTING HURDLE

My greatest quilting hurdle has been to get recognition for my machine quilting. Because much of the work I do is entered or displayed in quilt shows in the two-person category, the maker of the top is often listed as the winner, without mention of the person who quilted it. Plus, there is usually only one ribbon to share. This has been true of some of the major shows as well as the local shows. This is a fairly new phenomenon since it has been only in the last ten years the two-person categories were created. Paving the way for longarm machine quilters around the world has been one of the most frustrating aspects of my quilting career.

Patricia Maixner Magaret & Donna Ingram Slusser

Pam Bono Designs

Patrick Lose

Ruth B. McDowell

2000

Lerlene Nevaril

🔲 *Favorite* QUILTING TIP

ONE OF THE MOST IMPORTANT TIPS I GIVE TO MY STUDENTS IS THE USE OF A SCRAP OF STARTER FABRIC IN THE SEWING MACHINE. BENEFITS ARE THREE-FOLD:

1. IT PREVENTS THREADS FROM DRAWING INTO THE MACHINE AND CAUSING JAMS
2. IT ELIMINATES THREAD TAILS TO CUT AND PICK UP OFF THE FLOOR
3. IT SAVES THREAD.
I CAN'T SEW WITHOUT ONE!

SIGNIFICANT CHANGES IN THE LAST 20 YEARS

The rotary cutter has had a great impact on the quilting world—it revolutionized my quilting experience. Suddenly my pieces were all the same size and on grain. I could put together a block quickly and accurately. If you took away my rotary cutter, I'd have to go back to needlepoint!

Gwen Marston

FAVORITE QUILTING QUOTE

WHEN IN DOUBT, MAKE A NINE-PATCH.

PROUDEST QUILTING EXPERIENCE

I learned to quilt from a group of elderly Mennonite women. I have always felt that they gave me a gift for life. They taught me a skill that has played a central role in my life. My friendship with Mary Schafer has enriched my life and formed my attitudes and approach to quilting. Mary is a great Michigan quilter whose quilts are now housed permanently at the Michigan State University Museum.

Darlene Christopherson

SIGNIFICANT CHANGES IN THE LAST 20 YEARS

Quiltmaking has evolved in the past 20 years to reflect the lives of the women and men who love the craft. Occupations are more demanding and families are pressed for leisure time. Stitching by hand is a compelling source of relaxation.

🔲 *Favorite* QUILTING TIP

NEVER UNDERESTIMATE THE VALUE OF AN ACCURATE TEMPLATE FOR PATCHWORK. ENJOY THE PROCESS OF DRAFTING YOUR OWN PATTERNS. PRESERVING HAND STITCHERY CAN BE A REWARDING EFFORT. IN THIS MODERN DAY OF MACHINES THAT CAN DO ALL THE WORK FOR YOU, SERENITY AWAITS YOU IN THE COMFORT OF YOUR FAVORITE CHAIR.

Terrell Sundermann

Diane Phalen

Joen Wolfrom

Judith Baker Montano

2000

Claudia Olson

FAVORITE QUILTING STORY

Last year my Round Robin group decided to put on a skit for our quilt guild. What started out as a way of showing the evolution of a quilt group, turned out to be a hilarious comedy. We started our skit by drawing our patterns on fabric with a pencil and used cardboard templates, which we threw over our shoulder when we finished. One of our members surprised us by popping in to show us a new invention, a rotary cutter. After that miraculous invention, we proceeded to produce mass quantities of quilts. My character had hot flashes and kept mopping her face, fanning her dress and throwing off articles of clothing, which another woman who was too cold would grab up and hastily put on. Another quilter had to use a giant magnifying glass to thread her needle, which she continued to lose. One woman could not hear, and she mixed up everything we said, embarrassing us all. The funniest woman, who in real life is a judge, turned into a kleptomaniac. She went around the table stealing fabric, shawls, and cookies. We brought the house down with laughter and had great fun in the process!

GREATEST QUILTING HURDLE

The invention of computer design programs was helping me design quilts at incredible speed, but I could not keep up with the stitching. I was at a loss as to how to proceed. Then my quilting friends stepped up to help me. One after another they took patterns home and came back with samples to show me. I began to see my ideas and dreams come to life. I was overwhelmed to see the finished quilts and struck with the thought of "Oh my gosh, my designs are real now, not just a dream."

The journey to move from quilt designer to author has been exciting and very fulfilling. It has made me realize how many good friends I have and how much I appreciate them. They made it possible for me to achieve my high goals and they did it with willing, helpful spirits.

Susan Carlson

Barbara Brackman

Lynette Jensen

Jane A. Sassaman

2000

Joyce Becker

FAVORITE QUILTING STORY

Long, long, ago, (well, maybe ten years ago), in a land far, far away (60 miles as the crow flies), I loaded my van with my quilting buddies and their assorted quilting paraphernalia and whisked them away to a magical quilting retreat.

While cruising along the highway toward our enchanted destination, my demonic, menopausal, alter-personality entered my body—replacing my normal, easygoing, happy personality—as the mother of all hot flashes crept stealthily up my neck. With outside temperatures hovering in the forties, I rolled down my window and flipped on the air vent. With sweat pouring off my brow, I recklessly began flinging off clothing. Frantic, I finally switched the air vent to max and I began to cool down. Once I regained my composure I glanced into the rear view mirror, only to notice my quilting buddies had all pulled on their heavy winter coats and were huddled together, shivering under a car throw, uttering nary a peep. Now on HRT (Hormone Replacement Therapy), my sweet, wonderful, likable personality returned!

PROUDEST QUILTING EXPERIENCE

The spiritual part of me believes that each of us is put on earth for a purpose. I didn't discover my purpose for a very long time. Now that I have, my life is rich and complete. The pride I feel when my students and peers take the methods I share with them and create beautiful, unique landscape quilts is indescribable. When that "invisible light bulb" goes on for a student and they create without fear, soaring to new and exciting heights, my heart genuinely bursts with pride. There is no feeling on earth equal to this sense of satisfaction.

2000

Liz Aneloski

FAVORITE C&T STORY

After being a stay-at-home mom for ten years, I decided it was time to go back to work part time. A phone call to C&T in 1991 looking for proofreading opportunities has turned into a full-time editing career. You never know what lies just around the corner.

Favorite QUILTING TIP

MY FAVORITE QUILTING TIP IS ACTUALLY A PIECE OF ADVICE I RECEIVED FROM JEAN WELLS. SHE TOLD ME NOT TO PLAN ON LARGE BLOCKS OF TIME TO QUILT. IF YOU PLAN TO SEW OR DESIGN FOR FIFTEEN MINUTES AT ANY GIVEN TIME, IT IS EASY TO FIT QUILTING INTO EVEN THE BUSIEST SCHEDULE AND INVARIABLY, THE FIFTEEN MINUTES TURNS INTO A LONGER AMOUNT OF TIME. EVENTUALLY THE PROJECT IS COMPLETED. THIS ADVICE HAS MADE IT POSSIBLE FOR ME TO CONTINUE TO FINISH QUILTS WHILE WORKING AS A FULL-TIME EDITOR AT C&T. IT HAS EVEN ENABLED ME TO COMPLETE MY FIRST BOOK. THANK YOU, JEAN, FOR THE FABULOUS ADVICE!

Alice L. Dunsdon

Favorite QUILTING TIP

NEVER BE IN A HURRY. TAKE IT SLOW AND ENJOY THE PROCESS. YOU WILL HAVE FEWER MISTAKES AND LESS FRUSTRATION.

PROUDEST QUILTING EXPERIENCE

My proudest quilting moment is when I discovered that I could quilt without marking. I had enjoyed every aspect of the quilting process except the marking. When I crossed that hurdle (which I describe in my book *Fantastic Fans*) my joy was complete.

Gloria Hansen

Judy Heim & Gloria Hansen

Gloria Hansen

Judy Heim & Gloria Hansen

Susanna Oroyan

2001

Flavin Glover

FAVORITE QUILTING STORY

One of my favorite quilting stories occurred while I was interviewing quilt-makers in 1981.

The Henderson Quilting Club was established in 1946. Originally, their goal with quilting was to raise funds for the upkeep of Hopewell Cemetery in Henderson, Alabama. In 1970, they moved the quilting to the Pike Pioneer Museum to demonstrate and educate. For fifteen years, you could find Essie Berry, 88, over a quilt frame at the Museum five days a week from 10 A.M.–4 P.M. She readily admitted, quilting was a major part of her life, and had been for some time. Her Basket quilt, made in 1914, was on display at the Museum.

Elizabeth Richburg Johnson, 84, usually worked to Essie's right and drove her to the Museum every day.

Elizabeth was familiar with most of the names of the quilts on display and prided herself in naming them: Fence Rail, Trip Around the World, Friendship quilt. Others joined in, recognizing one as a Log Cabin (a black and red Barn Raising).

Elizabeth quickly spoke up, "That don't look like a Log Cabin to me. Don't call it Log Cabin if it ain't a Log Cabin."

Essie intervened, "Elizabeth, you know that's a Log Cabin. We've been calling that quilt Log Cabin for years."

Elizabeth snapped back, "I hadn't, and won't start today. I'll call it a stack of lumber. That's all that is, a stack of lumber, a Log Cabin quilt ought to look like a Log Cabin."

I chuckle when reviewing the exchange of words and hope that when I am 84 I will be sitting around a quilt frame as opinionated and frisky as Elizabeth was over two decades ago.

SIGNIFICANT CHANGES IN THE LAST 20 YEARS

I marvel at what has changed. Walk into a quilt show or conference and listen to the sounds. The enthusiasm, interest, anticipation, and sense of community are as alive today as in the early 1980s. We haven't gotten "glazed over."

We share a common bond (disease) that brings unlikely souls together. Quiltaholism reaches beyond age, socio-economic, and educational barriers. Whether young or old, rich or poor, brilliant or only above average, quiltaholism can and will strike. We are still buying fabric like crazy and just as delusional regarding getting it cut and sewn back together in our lifetime. What fun!

Sally Collins

Katie Pasquini Masopust

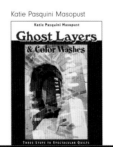

Alex Anderson

Alex Anderson

Alex Anderson

2001

Lynette Young Bingham

FAVORITE QUILTING STORY

In 2001, when I was a student in one of my mother's (Blanche Young) classes, the lady sitting next to me was a new quilter, having started a year before. She said that she overheard her husband boasting to some of his friends about the quilts she had made. He said, "If that $20 she spends on fabric makes her happy, I'm all for it!"

 Favorite QUILTING TIP

I RECENTLY PURCHASED ONE OF THE NEW, WIDE IRONING BOARDS. NOT QUITE WILLING TO PART WITH MY 32-YEAR-OLD WEDDING-GIFT IRONING BOARD, I ADJUSTED THE HEIGHT OF MY SEWING TABLE, AND PLACED THE BOARD BEHIND IT. IT EXTENDED MY WORKSPACE, WHICH REALLY CAME IN HANDY WHEN MACHINE QUILTING.

Early Quilt

Recent Quilt

Ann Frischkorn & Amy Sandrin

Jean & Valori Wells

Jennifer Sampou & Carolyn Schmitz

Mary Mashuta

Mary Lou Weidman

2001

Barbara Barber

FAVORITE QUILTING QUOTE

IF YOU FAIL TO PREPARE, BE PREPARED TO FAIL.

 Favorite QUILTING TIP

WHEREVER POSSIBLE, USE STARCH TO IMPROVE THE EASE OF WORK AND THE QUALITY OF THE FINISHED ARTICLE. WASH THE QUILTS WHEN COMPLETED, TO IMPROVE THE APPEARANCE.

Peggy Martin

SIGNIFICANT CHANGES IN THE LAST 20 YEARS

When I took my first quilting class, we did it all by hand using templates. All piecing was done by hand. It usually took me a whole day to cut out one block, and at least a couple days to hand piece it. All quilting was also by hand—machine quilting was either unheard of or greatly looked down upon. By the time I took my second class, I was taught to assembly-line piece, and rotary cutters were just beginning to be used. I could now make a block in just a few hours instead of days. Quick methods with the same accurate results—I was hooked! I've never gone back to the slow old ways, and am always looking for more efficient, fast, fun ways to piece and quilt. I'm also delighted that machine quilting is now accepted, because it gives me time to make more quilts!

 Favorite QUILTING TIP

KEEP AN OPEN MIND, DEVELOP A PLAYFUL ATTITUDE, AND VIEW MISTAKES AS NEW DESIGN OPPORTUNITIES. REALIZE THAT THERE IS NEVER ONLY ONE RIGHT ANSWER TO ANY QUILTING PROBLEM; THERE ARE MANY POSSIBILITIES. SO MANY TIMES WE BEGIN A QUILT WITH A VISION OF HOW IT WILL LOOK WHEN WE ARE FINISHED, ONLY TO DISCOVER THE END RESULT IS COMPLETELY DIFFERENT! ALWAYS BE OPEN TO EXPERIMENTATION WITH NEW COLOR COMBINATIONS, NEW SETTING IDEAS, AND NEW VARIATIONS TO WHAT YOU'VE DONE BEFORE.

Jan Krentz

Laura Lee Fritz

Marsha MacDowell, ed.

Carol Armstrong

Larraine Scouler

2001

Anita Grossman Soloman

FAVORITE QUILTING STORY

My husband is a prince, supportive and encouraging of all my endeavors, even when it involves literal intrusions into our lives like the floor to ceiling stacks of fabric that have slowly but surely come to fill every nook and cranny in our bedroom and closets. When I told him one day how much I appreciate his tolerance for the fabrics that have taken over our home, I mentioned that I'd heard of certain quilters who had resorted to hiding fabric in the trunks of their cars. Without missing a beat, he smiled back at me and said he'd ask me to do the same except we do not have a car.

FAVORITE QUILTING EXPERIENCE

As a teacher, there isn't a quilting experience that can compare to the thrill of seeing students' work. The first time I walked into the City Quilter shop in New York City to teach a follow-up class, I was awestruck by what the students had done. Their work astonished me because it was more thoughtful and exuberant than I could ever have imagined. It thrilled me to see that they had taken the skills they learned in the class and then applied them to their chosen fabrics in magical ways.

Favorite QUILTING TIPS

JOHN FLYNN, QUILTER EXTRAORDINAIRE FROM MONTANA, SHARED HIS CLEVER IDEA WITH ME. HE MACHINE BASTES THE QUILT SANDWICH TOGETHER USING WATER-SOLUBLE THREAD. IT GIVES TERRIFIC RESULTS AND MAKES THE QUILTING SUCH A PLEASURE. I ALWAYS WASH AND DRY MY QUILTS BEFORE I BLOCK, TRIM, AND BIND THEM, AND THE WATER-SOLUBLE THREAD SIMPLY DISSOLVES AWAY DURING THE LAUNDERING.

I WASH AND DRY ALL OF MY COTTON FABRIC. THEN, I STARCH THEM USING BOTTLED LIQUID LAUNDRY STARCH, REFRIGERATE THEM, AND IRON THE DAYLIGHTS OUT OF THEM. IF I SEW BY HAND, I SKIP THE STARCHING. IRONING DAMP FLANNEL IS A STEAMY ORDEAL, SO I SIMPLY ELIMINATE THE IRONING! I FOUND THAT DAMP, STARCHED FLANNEL WILL STICK TO MY HUSBAND'S NON-POROUS SHOWER WALL. WHEN DRY, I REMOVE THE TAUT FLANNEL FROM THE SHOWER WALL. I WIPE OFF ANY FUZZ LEFT ON THE TILE WHEN I SHOWER, SINCE MY BATHTUB WAS CALLED INTO SERVICE FOR FABRIC STORAGE LONG AGO.

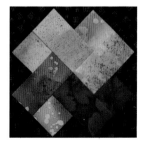

Nancy Johnson-Srebro

Jan Mullen

Paula Nadelstern

Laurel Burch

Yvonne Porcella

2001

Elly Sienkiewicz

Elly has written sixteen needlework books on appliqué. Twelve of her books are on Baltimore Album quilts; eleven of them comprise the Baltimore Beauties and Beyond series, begun in 1989. Elly places a complex historical style—the Baltimore-style Album quilts—within the grasp of every contemporary quiltmaker through her clear patterns and techniques, which demystify the construction process.

A history major with a lifetime love of needleart, Elly's traditionalist spirit desired to stay at home once her children began to arrive. She was led to home-centered enterprises, eventually those relating to the burgeoning quilt industry. Her experiences ranged from quilting teacher to retail mail-order proprietress, to respected quiltmaker, to author and historian. Since 1996 she has presided over the annual Elly Sienkiewicz Appliqué Academy (www.EllySienkiewicz.com), now in Williamsburg, Virginia.

Susan McKelvey

Susan McKelvey is a quilt artist, teacher, and the author of several books on quilting on quilts. Her great love in quilting is color and helping quilters to use color effectively in their work. *A Treasury of Quilt Labels* grew out of Susan's interest in writing on quilts and was inspired by the creativity of the quilters she has met through her traveling and teaching.

Susan has been quilting since 1977. Her work has appeared in museums, galleries, and quilt shows throughout the United States, as well as in magazines and books. In 1987 she began her own company, Wallflower Designs, to design and produce supplies and patterns for quilters who want to write on quilts.

Katie Pasquini Masopust

Katie has traveled all over the world teaching contemporary quilt design. She has changed her style over the years, starting with traditional works, then creating mandalas, followed by dimensional quilts. She enjoys landscapes, and feels as if she has returned full circle to her beginning as a painter; now she paints with fabric.

Katie has won many awards throughout her career including Best of Show at the Houston Quilt Festival in 1982 and 1986, and at the Pacific International Quilt Show 1994, and First and Second at the AQS Show 1995. Her piece *Dimensional Portal* was in the 1991 Quilt National and won the People's Choice award. Recently, *Passages, Chaco Canyon* won the Penny Nii award at the 1998 Visions Show.

Gai Perry

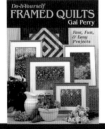

Cyndy Lyle Rymer, ed.

Sharyn Craig

Wendy Hill

Louisa L. Smith

2001

Pepper Cory

Pepper has been quilting since 1972. She saw an antique quilt at a rummage sale, purchased the quilt for $1 and has been making quilts, collecting antique quilts, teaching quilting, and writing quilt books ever since.

Becky Schaefer

Becky Schaefer began quiltmaking in 1972 and taught her approach to machine-pieced miniature quilts on both the East and West coasts and in Japan. Her award-winning work has been shown in a variety of publications.

Kathy Pace

For many years, Kathy Pace has been creating garments and a whole menagerie of wonderfully dressed toys and pets for her Gooseberry Hill mail-order company. She is the owner and primary designer, and has done most of the designing, photography, set-up, and instructional work.

Charlotte Patera

Charlotte's interest in appliqué produced an ardent curiosity about the molas of the Kuna Indians of the San Blas Islands in Panama. She sought out accurate mola methods by visiting the San Blas Islands on five occasions—not as a tourist, but as a needlewoman sharing ideas with the Indian mola makers.

Charlotte Warr Andersen

After being thoroughly immersed in many of the needle arts for her first three decades, quiltmaking and teaching the processes for making art quilts has become Charlotte's career of choice. She started out making traditional quilts and soon came to realize the pictorial and representational possibilities inherent in the fabric medium.

Cheryl Greider Bradkin

Cheryl grew up in the San Francisco Bay Area and had an early introduction to the textiles of many cultures through her mother's collection of ethnic clothing. She began sewing Seminole patchwork in 1977 and found the technique successfully combined the precision of her scientific education with her love of color and fabric.

Judith Baker Montano

2001

Kristen Dibbs
2001

Karey Bresenhan
2002

Harriet Hargrave

2002

Joen Wolfrom

Joen began quiltmaking in 1974 after she left her career in the educational field to become a homemaker. Her interest in color and design surfaced in the early 1980s. During that time, Joen challenged herself to experiment with new techniques and visual ideas. She is noted for being the innovator of several techniques, including strip-pieced landscapes and organic curved designs. Joen has taught and lectured in the quilting field, both nationally and internationally, since 1984. Her work is included in collections throughout the world.

Ruth B. McDowell

Ruth is an internationally known quilt artist, teacher, lecturer, and author. She has made over 300 quilts during the last two decades. Her quilts have been seen in many solo shows, as well as in dozens of magazines and books.

As she continues with the process of making quilts, interests change, themes weave in and out, ideas percolate for a while, then suddenly burst to the surface when the time seems right. Her best quilts happen through a process that is nonverbal, and usually not logical in any commonly accepted sense of the word. But a conjunction of things seen, heard, and felt with fabrics, patterns, and images starts a conversation that is recorded in a quilt.

Virginia Avery

A self-taught quilt and clothing designer, Virginia Avery has been professionally active in the quilt world for many years. She has been featured as teacher, lecturer, and judge at major quilt conferences, guilds, universities, and art museums throughout the world. Virginia brings warmth and wit to her work, and shares enthusiasm and information without reservation. Her perception of individual creative needs ensures enthusiastic response from her students. Her award-wining work is represented in many public and private collections; among her one-woman shows are the Smithsonian Institute and the Textile Museum of Washington, D.C. For rest and relaxation, Virginia plays piano for an eight-man Dixieland Jazz band, the King Street Stompers. She feels strongly that jazz, quilting, and clothing design are sisters under the skin, for they are always improving on a theme.

Jean Ray Laury

Ruth B. McDowell

Trice Boerens

Jennifer Rounds & Cyndy Lyle Rymer, ed.

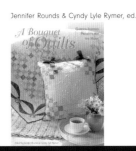

Kristina Becker

2002

Susanna Oroyan

Susanna taught herself the art of doll making. Since 1972, she has made over 500 dolls, and her doll making has become a full-time career and business. For the past decade, Susanna has been a motivating force in regional and national doll maker's organizations. She has exhibited her dolls internationally, and in 1995 received the Dollmaker of the Year award at the National Cloth Doll Festival.

Gai Perry

Gai was introduced to quilting in 1981 and fell head-over-heels in love with this uniquely American craft. She has been a full-time quilter ever since.

In 1985, Gai started teaching and, because of her fondness for early American quilts, her focus was on the effective use of color and fabric in traditional-style quilts. By 1990 she had a desire to start painting again, but instead of working with brushes and paint, she developed an original style of quilting she named "The Art of the Impressionist Landscape." She has written two books on the subject. Now Gai has temporarily returned to traditional quilting to write an exciting new lesson book filled with all kinds or practical and personal information about color and fabric.

Dalene Young Stone

As the youngest of Blanche Young's daughters, Dalene has always had sewing and fabrics as a part of her life. Dalene remembers sharing a bedroom with a sewing machine, and many nights being lulled to sleep by the hum of the machine as her mother worked. At age thirteen, Dalene received her first sewing machine (although at the time she secretly wished the box contained a stereo) and she made her first quilt—a *Lone Star*—when she was sixteen. Dalene admits to failing Home Economics, due to the fact that she insisted on doing things the way her mother taught her—not how the teacher wanted things done.

Cozy Baker

Kathy Sandbach

Diana McClun & Laura Nownes

Jean & Valori Wells

Jean Wells & Lawry Thorn

2002

Nancy Crow

Nancy has always thought long and hard about what she wanted to accomplish with her work. What became apparent was that she wanted to reach a state where work would flow out of her unimpeded, freely, joyously, and that it would represent whoever she was and her experiences. Long ago, she quit caring that fabric was not a particularly acceptable medium in the art world, because caring meant a denial of what she loved. This relaxed attitude released a lot of energy. It seemed to her that the only way to work was to think of fabric as her ally.

Carol Armstrong

Carol taught herself to quilt in 1980, developing her unique and highly artistic style. Botanically correct conventionalized celebrations of flora, birds, and woodland creatures are her favorite subject, though any object that catches her artistic eye may end up a minutely detailed grace on fabric.

Carol says wonderfully snowy winters give her time to do lots of quilting while her husband "Red" makes fine craft items in his workshop a path away. When her fingers and eyes need a diversion, there is always water to pump and bring in the house, wood to load in the woodbox, bird feeders to fill, or the large organic vegetable garden to tend.

Barbara Brackman

Barbara lives in Lawrence, Kansas, a town that was at the heart of Bleeding Kansas in the years before the Civil War. She is a historian who is immersed in the mid-nineteenth century, curating exhibits for various museums on topics from quiltmaking and the sewing machine to cowboy boots. With Terry Clothier Thompson, she designs reproduction cotton fabrics for Moda. She has written numerous books on quiltmaking and history.

Carol Armstrong

Jennifer Chiaverini & Nancy Odom

Kim Churbuck

Dilys A. Fronks

Elly Sienkiewicz

2002

Diana Leone

Diana's first quilts were the "Earth" series made for her Master's Exhibit at San Jose State University in 1973. She taught art in the public school system for thirteen years while raising her two sons. In 1975, she opened the Quilting Bee in Los Altos, California, which is currently located in Mountain View.

Patty McCormick

Never realizing where her interest in antiques and quilts would take her, Patty has since brought her enthusiasm and knowledge to the quilting community and the world at large. She was a ready and available resource for the movie industry's query into the art of quiltmaking, for *How to Make an American Quilt,* a call to which she eagerly responded.

Candace Kling

Candace's years of research in antique ribbon work and fabric embellishment explore both private and museum costume and textile collections across the country. Her highly detailed textile sculptures have been exhibited in museums and galleries, both nationally and internationally, and have earned her inclusion in the permanent collection of the American Craft Museum in New York City.

Celia Y. Oliver

As Curator of the Textiles Collections at the Shelburne Museum in Vermont, Celia supervises the research, exhibition, and publication of the quilt and bedcover collections. This collection illustrates the range of needlework and patterns used in the eighteenth and nineteenth-century.

Michael James

Michael is internationally recognized as one of the leading innovators in quilt-making today. For the last 20 years, he has devoted himself to exploring the creative possibilities inherent in the pieced quilt.

Deidre Scherer

During the mid-60s, Deidre studied painting at the Rhode Island School of Design. She developed a distinct narrative approach to fiber working with fabric and thread. She has addressed the issue of aging and mortality by building a series of images based on elders in her community.

Kathy MacMannis

Velda E. Newman

Carol Armstrong

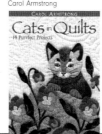

Lynette Jensen

2002

Amy Barickman

Amy's experience began with the influence of talented individuals, including her mother and grandmother. In high school, Amy enjoyed designing and making teddy bears. Upon graduation from college, She began an ambitious undertaking: marketing and selling patterns that she, her mother, and other designers created.

Ruth Reynolds

Ruth's busy hands had to sew *something*, so she took up quilting as a *hobby*, and before long she was consumed. Her quilts were always lively, funky, and *fun*. Before long, Ruth met up with Riva and created the Riva series of cartoon quilts, which travel all over the country to both quilt shows and galleries.

Cozy Baker

Cozy is internationally recognized as the First Lady of Kaleidoscopes because of the many firsts she has introduced: writing the first book on the subject, curating the nation's first kaleidoscope exhibition, and forming the world's first organization for kaleidoscope enthusiasts (the Brewster Society) in honor of Sir David Brewster, the scope's inventor.

Mimi Ayers

Mimi Ayers began quilting in 1974, and she is now engaged in a career of writing for quilt magazines, professional journals, and newsletters. She is also an instructor and speaker on various topics including quilts, the women who made them, and their history.

Freddy Moran

I believe every person needs a passion; be it tennis or golf, or gardening . . . whatever one finds as an inner core to keep them vital and interested, and I hope interesting. Age fades and creativity takes over—what a powerful feeling.

Jennifer Gilbert

Jennifer Gilbert is the curator of the New England Quilt Museum in Lowell, MA. As a child she visited many museums here and abroad. Studying the evolution of the quilt has provided her a fascinating look into the artistic lives of American quiltmakers both past and present.

Joen Wolfrom

Oklahoma Embroidery Supply & Design

Lerlene Nevaril

Marie-Christine Flocard & Cosabeth Parriaud

Laura Lee Fritz

2002

Patrick Lose

Patrick has spent his professional years in a variety of creative fields. He began his career as an actor and singer, which eventually led him to design costumes for stage and screen. His costume credits include more than 50 productions and work with celebrities such as Liza Minelli and Jane Seymour.

An artist and illustrator since childhood, Patrick works in many mediums. When he sits down to "doodle" at the drawing board, he never knows what one of his designs might become. Whether it's designing fabric for his collections or working on designs for quilts, wearable art, cross-stitch, greeting cards, Christmas ornaments, or home décor, he enjoys creating it all.

Mickey Lawler

Mickey Lawler and her SKYDYES have become synonymous with the finest individually hand-painted fabrics available to quilt and fiber artists. Her fabrics have been used as a design focus in quilts by many of today's most illustrious quiltmakers.

In 1980 she opened a quilt shop and soon began dyeing, then painting, cotton to satisfy her own need for landscape and textural fabrics. When it quickly became apparent that other quiltmakers were drawn to her fabric, Mickey sold her shop, turning her energies, and passion, to painting fabric full time. Since that time she also has been in demand as an enthusiastic instructor for teaching her serendipitous style of fabric painting.

Pat Magaret and Donna Slusser

Pat and Donna both started as traditional quiltmakers in the early 1980s after a lifetime of sewing and crafting. They soon branched out from tradition and began experimenting with color and design. They each began taking familiar blocks and using then in unique and innovative ways. Each brings different views and techniques to almost every subject and method. Pat is methodical, organized, prefers to design on graph paper, and is known for her beautiful hand quilting. Donna uses the "what would happen if I tried . . ." method, experimenting with the hands-on approach to fabric and design, and is a machine quilter.

Quilter's Newsletter Magazine & Quiltmaker

Alex Anderson

Claudia Olson

Quilter's Newsletter Magazine & Quiltmaker

Linda V. Taylor

2002

Pam Bono

After many years in the quilting business, Pam Bono has learned to follow her own drummer. Pam's husband Robert takes an active part in helping with both sewing and designing. Their fresh approach and innovative concepts have quilters all over the country excited about these new designs.

Susan Delaney-Mech

Susan's love of sewing began as she sat on the floor beside her grandmother's treadle-operated sewing machine. In 1988, Susan brought together the love she has for medicine, quiltmaking, and writing and began her long-running column, *Rx for Quilters*, for *Quilt World* magazine.

Susan Carlson

Susan grew up in Wheaton, Maryland, just north of Washington, D.C. She feels it was a great place to grow up since school field trips usually went to the national museums. She also feels lucky to have wonderfully supportive parents who were able to indulge her and her sister, Heidi's, creative desires.

Terrell Sundermann

A self-taught sewer, Terrell tends to see a picture in a book and then "just make it." After making a log cabin wallhanging, Terrell began experimenting with combining a wallhanging and a Roman shade. Her background in physics proved valuable as she perfected the functional portion of window hangings.

Gül Laporte

Gül now lives in France but has lived in Algeria, Syria, Greece, the United States, and the United Kingdom. She is fluent in French, English, and Spanish and conversant in Greek. She originally discovered quilting in 1981 in Houston. Upon returning to Europe, she continued to quilt and soon began teaching throughout Europe.

Laurel Burch

After a move to the Haight-Ashbury district of San Francisco, Laurel began selling her hand-made jewelry in the streets and in small galleries. Laurel Burch's Kindred Creatures are just a small part of the magical world she has enjoyed creating. Through her thriving business, she pours her passion for color and all living creatures into her art.

Flavin Glover

Nancy Johnson-Srebro

Blanche Young & Lynette Young Bingham

Carol Armstrong

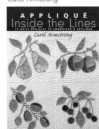

Joyce R. Becker

2003

Lynette Jensen

Lynette's company, Thimbleberries, publishes books and patterns about quilt making as well as lifestyle and decorating. She designs the popular Thimbleberries fabric line, consisting of cotton calicos, flannels, and woven plaids, for RJR Fashion Fabrics. Her publications and fabrics can be found in independent quilt shops worldwide. Her work is featured in major quilting publications and television shows.

Jan Krentz

Jan Krentz is an active member in the quilting community. She is a teacher, designer, pattern maker, and author inspiring others to enjoy the art of quilt-making. Jan started sewing at an early age, and is skilled in a variety of needlework disciplines.

Best known for her color selection and technical skill, Jan's quilts are beautifully distinctive. She began making quilts in 1973, and teaching the art of quiltmaking in 1982. She eagerly shares the art of quilting with all who will listen, and is a motivating teacher.

Velda Newman

Velda is a contemporary fiber artist from northern California. Her large-scale designs, portraying subjects from nature, have been exhibited extensively throughout the United States, Europe, and Japan. Velda uses textiles and thread the way other artists use paint and brush. Her primary source of inspiration is the world of nature, and her exquisitely crafted quilts reflect the detail she finds there. Her work has appeared in many national and international publications and is included in both public and private collections. Velda lectures and teaches quiltmaking in her own style of creating realism.

Valori Wells

Jean Wells

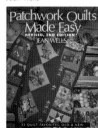

Jan Krentz

Cyndy Lyle Rymer, ed.

Jan Mullen

2003

Amy Sandrin and Ann Frischkorn

Amy and Ann are identical twins who, despite the thousand miles separating them, still manage to converse almost daily. Amy is an award-winning romance author who dabbles in quilting. Ann is an award-winning quilter who dabbles in writing. In one of their many conversations, they joked about combining both their talents and collaborating on a quilting book together.

The joke turned to reality when they discovered the flower pounding process, and knew it was their destiny to share this technique with the quilting and crafting world.

Jennifer Sampou and Carolyn Schmitz

Jennifer is a leading textile designer in the quilting industry. She has traveled the world gathering inspiration for her designs, and is known for her diverse hand and exceptional color sense.

Jennifer has a degree in Surface Design from the Fashion Institute of Technology in New York and a Bachelor of Science degree in Textiles from the University of Vermont. After serving as a Creative Director for P&B Textiles for seven years, she decided, at age thirty, that she was ready to start a family. In order to continue her career, she opened her own home-based business, Studio Sampou. Currently she licenses her designs to Robert Kaufman Company.

Carolyn is one of the most gifted and talented decorative painters working today in the southeastern Massachusetts and Rhode Island area. Her designs have been featured in such publications as *Victoria, Bon Appetit, Rhode Island Monthly, Cape Cod Life, Newport Life, The Bathroom Idea Book,* and *The Providence Journal Magazine.* She has been selected to participate in prestigious designer show houses throughout New England, and her own homes have been sought after for tours and been granted awards for historic preservation and paint colors. Carolyn has also designed children's furniture, and she recently collaborated on a line of children's fabric with her sister Jennifer.

Carolyn holds a Bachelor of Fine Arts from the University of Massachusetts–Amherst and Sir John Cass School of Art in London, and she continues to study art at the Rhode Island School of Design in Providence, Rhode Island.

Darlene C. Christopherson

Quilter's Newsletter Magazine & Quiltmaker

Alex Anderson

Peggy Martin

Cyndy Lyle Rymer & Jennifer Rounds

2003

Kristen Dibbs

Australian textile artist Kristen Dibbs began teaching her innovative approach to machine embroidery in 1987. Her magazine articles and books about machine embroidery have reached an international audience. Two examples of her original techniques for embroidered lace work are held in the Powerhouse Museum of Applied Arts in Sydney.

Laura Lee Fritz

Laura is widely known for her hand appliqué and fanciful wholecloth quilts filled with narrative images from the stories surrounding her life. She teaches quilting classes everywhere—from her weekly class at a local college to her longarm machine quilting classes at the annual International Quilt Festival in Houston.

Marsha MacDowell

Marsha's colleagues at the Michigan State University Museum share the passion of developing the museum's collection and engaging others in research and education activities related to quilts. Countless volunteers—both quilters and quilt lovers—have long been instrumental in building the collections and in carrying out the museum's quilt-related activities.

Kim Churbuck

Kim teaches and travels to quilt shows around the country. She has written several books of designs about quilt-label making. Kim lives in Iowa with a house full of creativity-inspiring animals—not the least of which are Sophie (a fox terrier) and Olivia (a Parson Russell terrier).

Kathy MacMannis

Kathy created the Rag Wool Embroidery™ technique, which allows her to create the illusion of rug hooking on her embroidery machine. She also works as an emergency room nurse.

Jennifer Chiaverini

Jennifer Chiaverini is the author of the Elm Creek Quilts novel series. She lives with her husband and son in Madison, Wisconsin, where she quilts with the Mad City Quilters.

Mary Mashuta

Ruth B. McDowell

Liz Aneloski

Gwen Marston

Elly Sienkiewicz

2003

Rita Hutchens

Primarily self-taught, with a strong determination to be unique, Rita makes her living as a professional artist creating and selling her work in beading and quilting, as well as teaching and writing about her inventive techniques in both disciplines.

Ricky Tims

Ricky is known in the international world of quilting as an enthusiastic and encouraging teacher, an award-winning quilter, and a talented and spellbinding speaker. His innovative and entertaining presentations feature live music and humor combined with scholarly insights.

Oklahoma Embroidery Supply & Design

OESD is a manufacturer and distributor of embroidery designs and professional quality stabilizers, threads and embroidery accessories. Their design catalog features over 20,000 embroidery designs. The company produces new embroidery designs and embroidery cards continually, adding innovative products to their line.

Jan Rapacz

Jan loves to experiment with every needlework technique that comes around. She has taught classes in smocking, tatting, and silk ribbon embroidery, and feels that teaching is a responsibility of any needleworker who wants to keep the techniques from becoming lost arts.

Kristin Steiner

It seems Kristin grew up with the quilt world, teaching herself at first, and then absorbing the latest techniques quiltmaking had to offer. She has her own pattern line, Straight From My Heart Designs, where she shares her unique design style, not quite folky but definitely not fussy, along with helpful tips for achieving beautiful appliqué.

Diane Frankenberger

Diane started quilting in the mid-60s after seeing a quilt in a *Time* magazine article on folk art. She thought, "I want to make that" and she did, poorly, with much help from store clerks, a neighbor, and her husband's aunt. Appliqué is her favorite with made up patterns (she can't read directions), but she loves all aspects of this art. She has no rules for others or herself but to do your best.

Rita Hutchens

Jan Rapacz
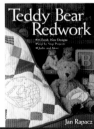

Ricky Tims

Kristin C. Steiner & Diane C. Frankenberger

Gai Perry

2003

Salley Mavor

Salley Mavor grew up in a household full of treasures and creative ideas in the seaside village of Woods Hole, Massachusetts. At home, there were always art supplies close-at-hand, and a sense that time was available for creative pursuit. Drawing with crayons was never enough for Salley. She remembers feeling that her work was not finished until something real was glued, stapled, or sewn to it.

A graduate of the Rhode Island School of Design, she has illustrated six children's books using her unique blend of materials and techniques. She now designs sewing kits and note cards for her business, Wee Folk Studio.

Becky Goldsmith and Linda Jenkins

Linda and Becky's friendship developed while they worked together on many guild projects and through a shared love for appliqué. This partnership led to the birth of Piece O' Cake Designs in 1994, and survived Linda's move to Pagosa Springs, Colorado, while Becky headed for Sherman, Texas.

Linda owned and managed a beauty salon before she started quilting. Over the years she developed a fine eye for color as a hair colorist and makeup artist. Becky's degree in interior design and many art classes provided a perfect background for quilting.

Salley Mavor

Nancy Smith & Lynda Milligan

Becky Goldsmith & Linda Jenkins

Becky Goldsmith & Linda Jenkins

Becky Goldsmith & Linda Jenkins

2003

Joyce Lytle

Joyce Lytle is C&T Publishing's senior technical editor, having been with the company since 1992. Since completing the National Quilters Association (NQA) Short Course on Quilt Judging in 1993, she has been judging quilt shows and fairs. She started quilting in 1980 and is very active in her local quilt guild, Diablo Valley Quilters.

Joyce has a degree in Home Economics Education from the State University of New York at Oneonta. She has taught junior high and high school Home Economics in New York State and California. She resides in San Ramon, California with her husband, Gary. They have two grown children.

Karey Bresenhan

Karey is the president of Quilts, Inc., director of International Quilt Market, International Quilt Festival, Patchwork & Quilt Expo, and Embellishment®. Karey's business acumen, enthusiasm for quilting, and perseverance helped her create and foster the quilting industry, now worth $1.84 billion a year in the U.S. She has been the driving force in fostering the growth of quilting in Europe, having started Expo there in 1988.

Karey is a fifth-generation Texas quilter and an acknowledged expert on quilt dating. She has served as a quilt appraiser and quilt contest judge. A personal quilt collection that includes family quilts, rare antique quilts, art quilts, and quilts made especially for her, testifies to Karey's love for this art form.

Mary Leman Austin

Mary Leman Austin was lucky enough to be born into the family of Bonnie and George Leman, the founders of *Quilter's Newsletter Magazine*. Mary has worked at the magazine since the tender age of thirteen, and upon her mother's retirement in 1996, took over as editor-in-chief of *QNM*. She lives in the Denver, Colorado area with Milt, her husband of 20 years, and their dog Bubba.

Linda Johansen

Liz Aneloski & Kandy Petersen, ed.

Alice Dunsdon

Anita Grossman Solomon

Jennifer Rounds & Catherine Comyns, ed.

2003

Blocks by C&T authors, setting by Sharyn Craig, machine quilted by Kathy Sandbach

Blocks by C&T authors, setting by Margaret Miller, machine quilted by Linda V. Taylor

Blocks by C&T authors, setting by Margaret Miller, machine quilted by Laura Lee Fritz

Blocks by C&T authors, setting by Sharyn Craig, machine quilted by Hari Walner

Author Challenge
BLOCK INFORMATION

Each of our authors was asked to contribute a block with the theme of Celebrations. They were given an 11" x 11" piece of C&T fabric and asked to include a portion of it in their block. The original fabric was printed on an off-white background. They were told that they could overdye, manipulate, or embellish it if they wished. The blocks that follow are the result of that challenge.

If you wish to duplicate the C&T fabric for your personal use, use the design on the inside front and back covers of this book and refer to *Imagery on Fabric* or *The Photo Transfer Handbook* for options on how to create your own image on fabric.

The quilts made using these blocks appear on pages 78–81.

Making and Using Templates

Pieced Blocks

MAKING TEMPLATES

1. Enlarge the block pattern to the desired size.

2. Label each piece of the block.

3. Place template plastic over the first piece. Trace a line around the piece using a fine-line permanent pen and ruler (sewing line).

4. Draw a line ¼" around the outside of the sewing line (cutting line).

5. Repeat for each piece of the block.

6. Cut out each template exactly down the center of the cutting line.

USING TEMPLATES

1. Trace each template onto the chosen fabrics using a fine-line permanent pen or chalk marker and ruler.

2. Cut out the pieces exactly down the center of the marked lines.

3. Sew the pieces together using a ¼" seam allowance.

Appliqué

MAKING FREEZER-PAPER TEMPLATES

1. Enlarge the block pattern to the desired size.

2. Label each piece of the appliqué.

3. On the **shiny** side of the freezer paper, trace a line around the first piece using a fine-line permanent pen (turn-under line).

4. Repeat for each piece of the appliqué shape.

5. Cut out each freezer-paper template exactly down the center of the turn-under line.

USING FREEZER PAPER TEMPLATES

1. Iron each template, shiny side down, onto the chosen fabrics.

2. Cut out the pieces ³⁄₁₆" outside the freezer-paper template.

3. Appliqué using your preferred method.

Machine Appliqué Using Fusible Adhesive

Note: Mirror image each appliqué shape, or it will be reversed from what appears in the book.

1. Lay the fusible web sheet paper-side up on the pattern and trace with a pencil. Trace detail lines with a permanent marker for ease in transferring to the fabric.

2. Use paper-cutting scissors to roughly cut out the pieces. Leave at least a ¼" border.

3. Following manufacturer's instructions, fuse the web patterns to the wrong side of the appliqué fabric. It helps to use an appliqué-pressing sheet to avoid getting the adhesive on your iron or ironing board.

4. Cut out the pieces along the pencil line. Do not remove the paper yet.

5. Transfer the detail lines to the fabric by placing the piece on a light table or up to the window and marking the fabric. Use pencil for this task—the lines will be covered by thread.

6. Remove the paper and position the appliqué piece on your project. Be sure the web (rough) side is down. Press in place, following the manufacturer's instructions.

Blocks

Enlarge 200% for 8" block, 225% for 9" block, 250% for 10" block, 275% for 11" block, and 300% for 12" block. See pages 82–83 for template and piecing instructions.

CAROLIE HENSLEY

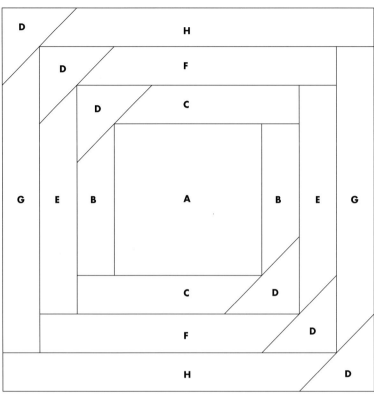

ROBERTA HORTON

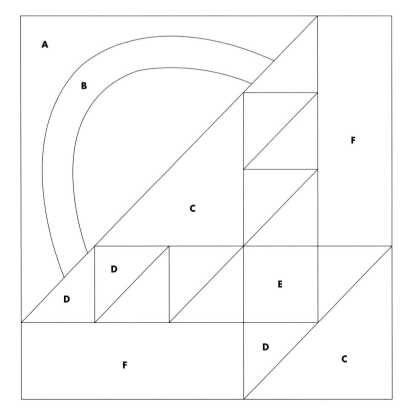

JUDITH BAKER MONTANO

Enlarge 200% for 8" block,
225% for 9" block,
250% for 10" block,
275% for 11" block,
and 300% for 12" block.
Refer to *Crazy Quilt Handbook, 2nd Edition*
for more detailed instructions for using the
Montano Center Piece crazy quilt method.

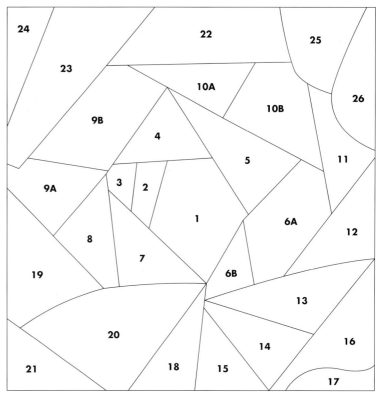

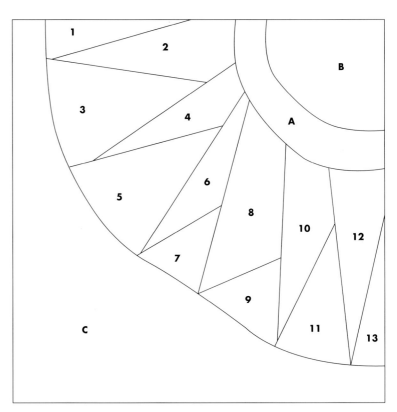

JEAN AND VALORI WELLS

Enlarge 200% for 8" block, 225% for 9" block, 250% for 10" block, 275% for 11" block, and 300% for 12" block. See pages 82–83 for template and piecing instructions. Refer to *Radiant New York Beauties* for more detailed instructions.

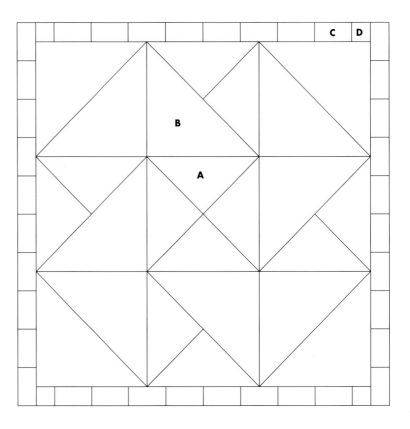

JEFFREY GUTCHEON

Enlarge 200% for 8" block, 225% for 9" block, 250% for 10" block, 275% for 11" block, and 300% for 12" block. See pages 82–83 for template and piecing instructions.

MARIANNE FONS

Enlarge 200% for 8" block, 225% for 9" block, 250% for 10" block, 275% for 11" block, and 300% for 12" block. See pages 82–83 for template and piecing instructions.

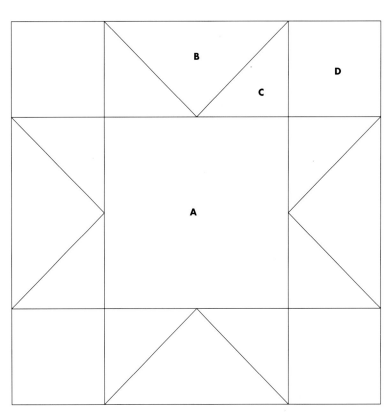

BLANCHE YOUNG

Enlarge 200% for 8" block, 225% for 9" block, 250% for 10" block, 275% for 11" block, and 300% for 12" block. See pages 82–83 for template and piecing instructions.

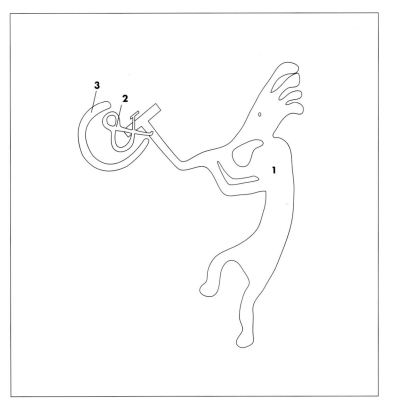

HELEN YOUNG FROST

Enlarge 200% for 8" block,

225% for 9" block,

250% for 10" block,

275% for 11" block,

and 300% for 12" block.

See pages 82–83 for template

and piecing instructions.

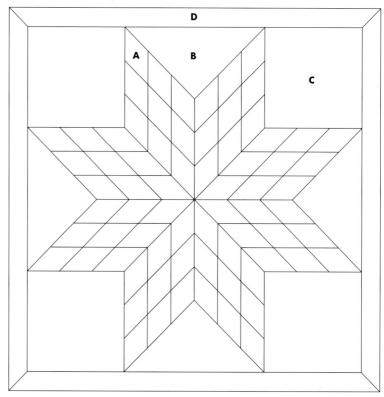

JUDY MATHIESON

DARLENE CHRISTOPHERSON

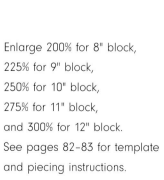

Enlarge 200% for 8" block,
225% for 9" block,
250% for 10" block,
275% for 11" block,
and 300% for 12" block.
See pages 82–83 for template
and piecing instructions.

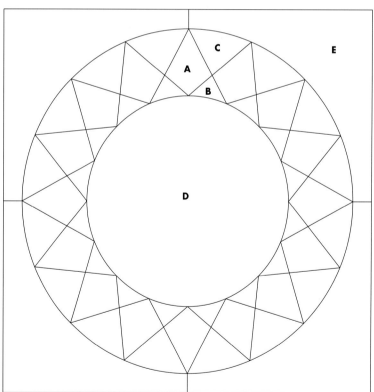

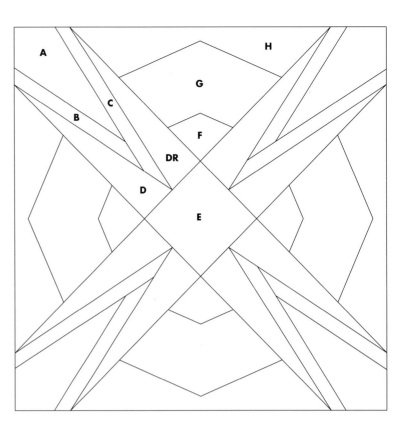

DIXIE HAYWOOD

Enlarge 200% for 8" block, 225% for 9" block,
250% for 10" block, 275% for 11" block,
and 300% for 12" block. See pages 82-83
for template and piecing instructions.

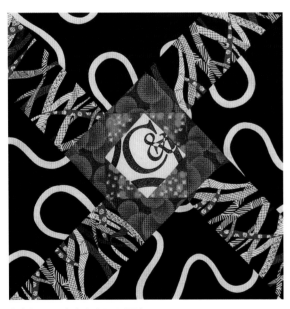

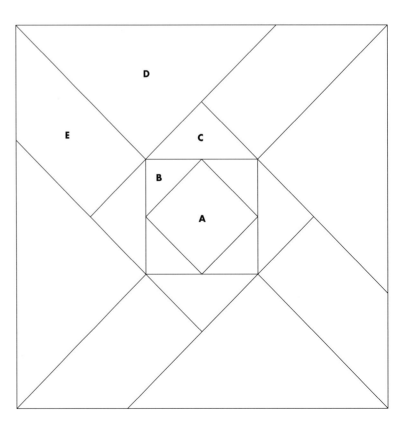

MARY MASHUTA

Enlarge 200% for 8" block, 225% for 9" block,
250% for 10" block, 275% for 11" block, and
300% for 12" block. See pages 82-83 for template
and piecing instructions.

JANE HALL

Enlarge 200% for 8" block,

225% for 9" block,

250% for 10" block,

275% for 11" block,

and 300% for 12" block.

See pages 82–83 for template and

piecing instructions. Optional: use your

favorite paper or fabric foundation

method. Make one quadrant four times

to create the block.

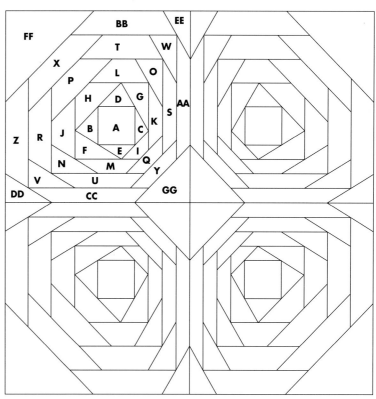

JEAN RAY LAURY

Enlarge 200% for 8" block, 225% for 9" block, 250% for 10" block, 275% for 11" block, and 300% for 12" block. Refer to *The Fabric Stamping Handbook* for more detailed instructions.

MIRIAM GOURLEY

Enlarge 200% for 8" block, 225% for 9" block, 250% for 10" block, 275% for 11" block, and 300% for 12" block. See page 83 for template and piecing instructions. Embroider straight stitches for hair.

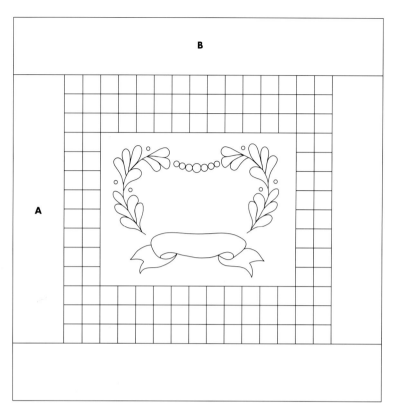

HARRIET HARGRAVE

Enlarge 200% for 8" block, 225% for 9" block, 250% for 10" block, 275% for 11" block, and 300% for 12" block. Refer to *Heirloom Machine Quilting* for more detailed instructions. See pages 82–83 for template and piecing instructions.

QUILT SAN DIEGO

Enlarge 200% for 8" block, 225% for 9" block, 250% for 10" block, 275% for 11" block, and 300% for 12" block. See pages 82–83 for template and piecing instructions.

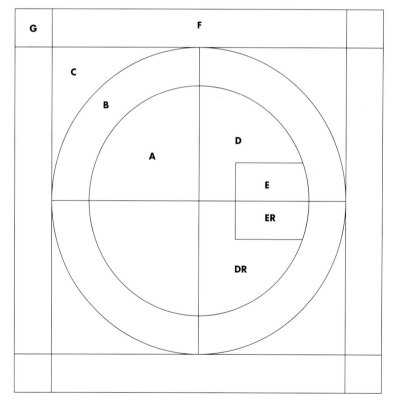

YVONNE PORCELLA

Enlarge 200% for 8" block,
225% for 9" block,
250% for 10" block,
275% for 11" block,
and 300% for 12" block.
Refer to *Magical Four-Patch* and *Nine-Patch Quilts* for more detailed instructions.

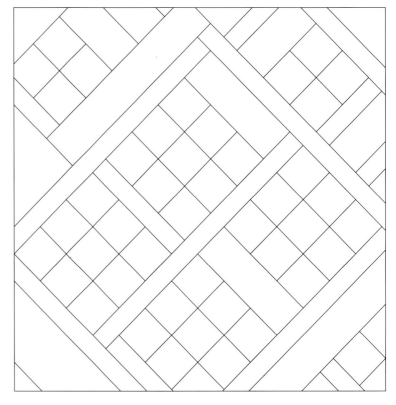

JINNY BEYER

Enlarge 200% for 8" block,
225% for 9" block,
250% for 10" block,
275% for 11" block,
and 300% for 12" block.
See pages 82–83 for template
and piecing instructions.

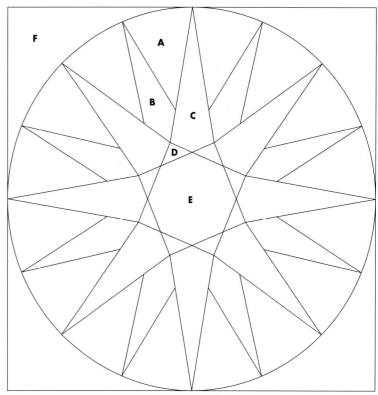

DIANA McCLUN AND LAURA NOWNES

Enlarge 200% for 8" block, 225% for 9" block, 250% for 10" block, 275% for 11" block, and 300% for 12" block. See page 83 for template and piecing instructions.

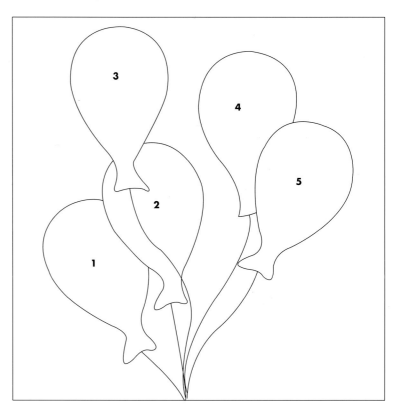

SHIRLEY NILSSON

Enlarge 200% for 8" block, 225% for 9" block, 250% for 10" block, 275% for 11" block, and 300% for 12" block. See pages 82–83 for template and piecing instructions.

RUTH B. McDOWELL

Enlarge 200% for 8" block,
225% for 9" block,
250% for 10" block,
275% for 11" block,
and 300% for 12" block.
See pages 82–83 for template and
piecing instructions. Use folded strips
of fabric for D2, E5, and E6.

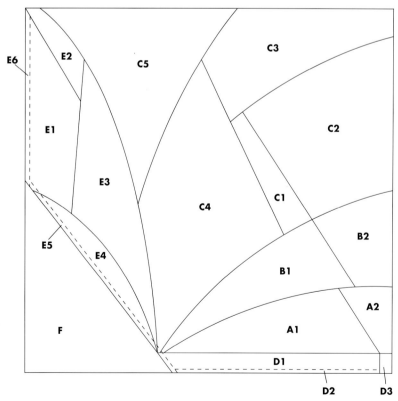

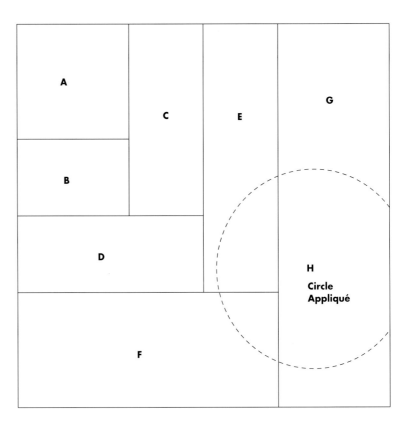

GAI PERRY

Enlarge 200% for 8" block, 225% for 9" block, 250% for 10" block, 275% for 11" block, and 300% for 12" block. See pages 82–83 for template and piecing instructions.

HARI WALNER

Enlarge 200% for 8" block, 225% for 9" block, 250% for 10" block, 275% for 11" block, and 300% for 12" block. See page 83 for template and piecing instructions. This view of Earth is impossible, but Hari felt everyone on the planet should be represented. She nudged and squeezed the continents. The C&T motif was placed every 30°.

SALLY COLLINS

Enlarge 200% for 8" block,
225% for 9" block,
250% for 10" block,
275% for 11" block,
and 300% for 12" block.
See pages 82–83 for template
and piecing instructions.

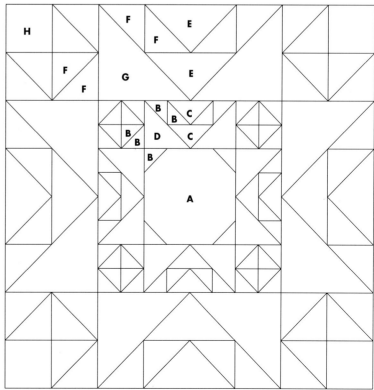

ALEX ANDERSON

Enlarge 200% for 8" block,
225% for 9" block,
250% for 10" block,
275% for 11" block,
and 300% for 12" block.
See pages 82–83 for template
and piecing instructions.

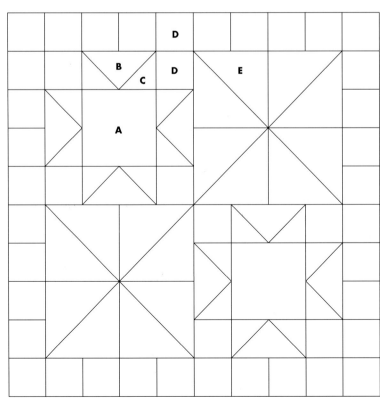

HELEN KELLEY

Enlarge 200% for 8" block,
225% for 9" block,
250% for 10" block,
275% for 11" block,
and 300% for 12" block.
See pages 82–83 for template
and piecing instructions.

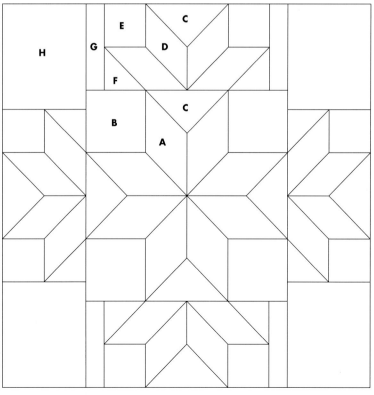

PAULA NADELSTERN

Enlarge 200% for 8" block,
225% for 9" block,
250% for 10" block,
275% for 11" block,
and 300% for 12" block.
See pages 82–83 for template and
piecing instructions. Use the same
bilaterally symmetrical fabric for
pieces A and C.

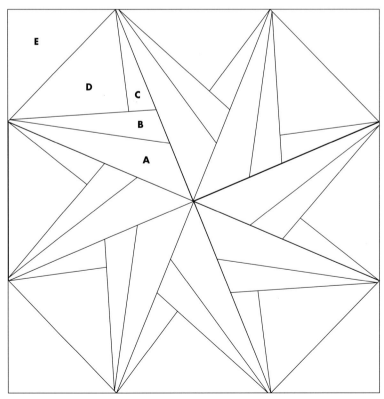

PAT CAMPBELL

Enlarge 200% for 8" block,
225% for 9" block,
250% for 10" block,
275% for 11" block,
and 300% for 12" block.
Refer to *Jacobean Rhapsodies* for more
information. See page 83 for template
and piecing instructions.

WENDY HILL

Enlarge 200% for 8" block, 225% for 9" block, 250% for 10" block, 275% for 11" block, and 300% for 12" block. Refer to *On the Surface* for more detailed instructions. Weaving strips should be cut 1" longer than the finished size of the block.

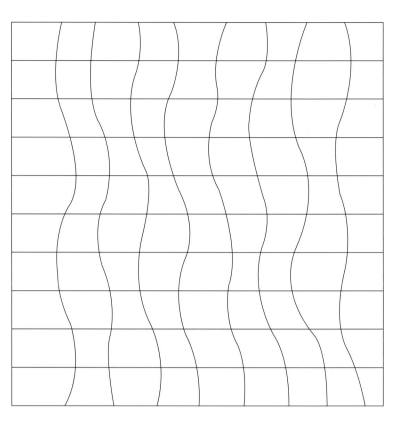

MARGARET MILLER

Enlarge 200% for 8" block, 225% for 9" block, 250% for 10" block, 275% for 11" block, and 300% for 12" block. See pages 82–83 for template and piecing instructions.

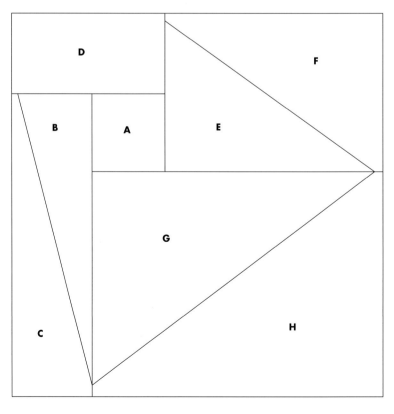

JUDY B. DALES

Enlarge 200% for 8" block,
225% for 9" block,
250% for 10" block,
275% for 11" block,
and 300% for 12" block.
 See pages 82-83 for template and
piecing instructions. Refer to *Curves in
Motion* for more detailed instructions.
Make one quadrant four times to create
the block. Sew the line between A and B
sections last.

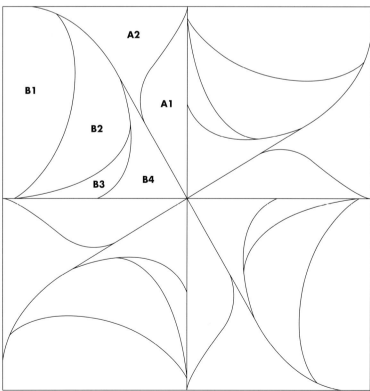

JUDY HEIM

Enlarge 200% for 8" block, 225% for 9" block, 250% for 10" block, 275% for 11" block, and 300% for 12" block. See page 83 for template and piecing instructions. The double thickness heart, gathered at the center, forms a pocket for fabric books attached with ribbon, bows, and wooden spools. Fill your heart with desired treasures.

GLORIA HANSEN

Enlarge 200% for 8" block, 225% for 9" block, 250% for 10" block, 275% for 11" block, and 300% for 12" block. See pages 82–83 for template and piecing instructions.

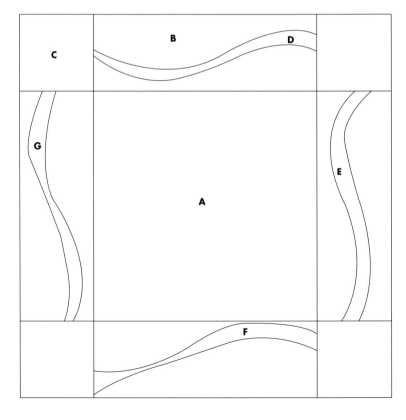

CAROL ARMSTRONG

Enlarge 200% for 8" block,
225% for 9" block,
250% for 10" block,
275% for 11" block,
and 300% for 12" block. See page 83
for template and piecing instructions.

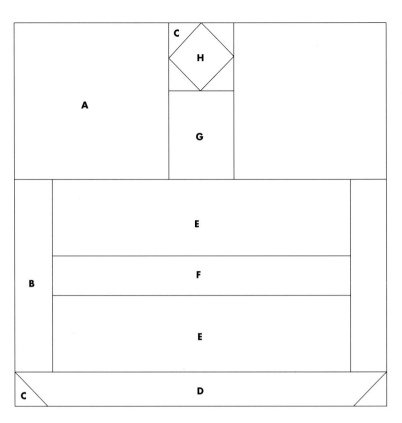

NANCY JOHNSON-SREBRO

Enlarge 200% for 8" block, 225% for 9" block, 250% for 10" block, 275% for 11" block, and 300% for 12" block. See pages 82–83 for template and piecing instructions.

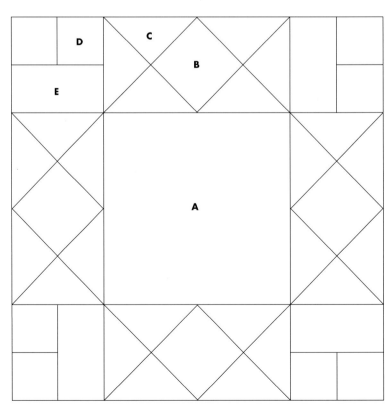

SHARYN CRAIG

Enlarge 200% for 8" block, 225% for 9" block, 250% for 10" block, 275% for 11" block, and 300% for 12" block. See pages 82–83 for template and piecing instructions.

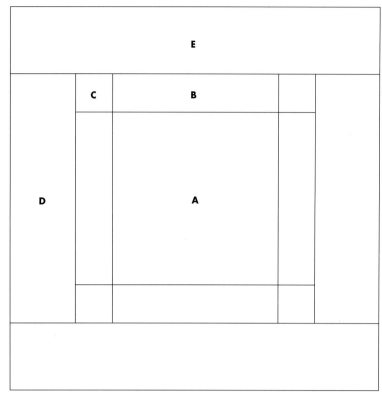

DIANE PHALEN

Enlarge 200% for 8" block, 225% for 9" block, 250% for 10" block, 275% for 11" block, and 300% for 12" block. See pages 82–83 for template and piecing instructions.

JANE A. SASSAMAN

Enlarge 200% for 8" block, 225% for 9" block, 250% for 10" block, 275% for 11" block, and 300% for 12" block. See page 83 for template and piecing instructions.

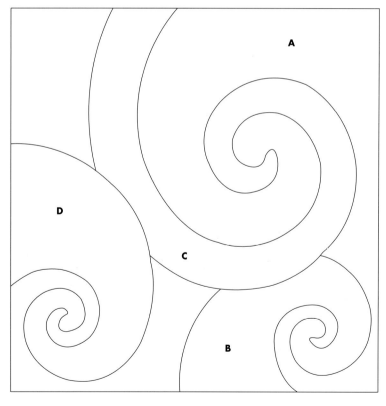

THE JIM HENSON COMPANY/ SESAME WORKSHOP, LAUREN ATTINELLO

Kermit the Frog™ appears courtesy of The Jim Henson Company. © 2002 The Jim Henson Company. JIM HENSON'S mark & logo, MUPPETS mark & logo, MUPPET, KERMIT THE FROG character and elements are trademarks of The Jim Henson Company. All Rights Reserved.

Enlarge 200% for 8" block,
225% for 9" block,
250% for 10" block,
275% for 11" block,
and 300% for 12" block.
Refer to *Quilting with the Muppets*
for more information. See page 83
for template and piecing instructions.

JENNIFER SAMPOU

Enlarge 200% for 8" block, 225% for 9" block, 250% for 10" block, 275% for 11" block, and 300% for 12" block. See page 83 for template and piecing instructions.

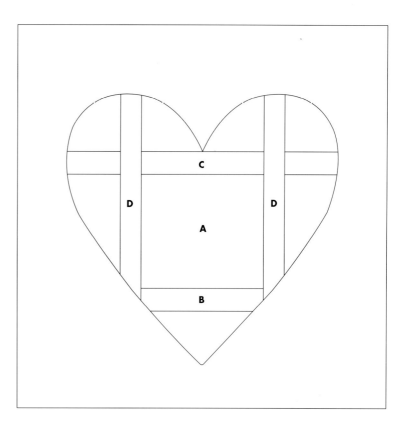

MARY LOU WEIDMAN

Enlarge 200% for 8" block, 225% for 9" block, 250% for 10" block, 275% for 11" block, and 300% for 12" block. See page 83 for template and piecing instructions.

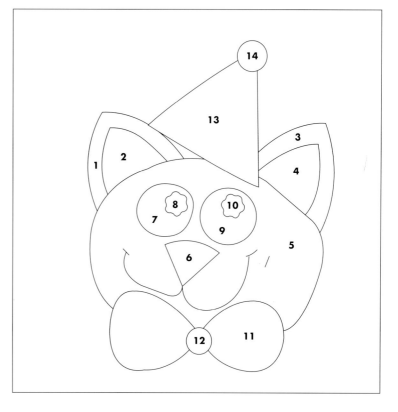

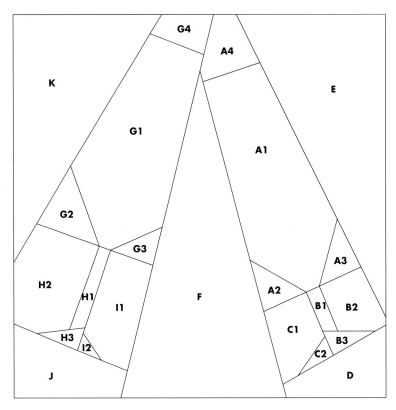

JAN MULLEN

Enlarge 200% for 8" block, 225% for 9" block, 250% for 10" block, 275% for 11" block, and 300% for 12" block. See pages 82–83 for template and piecing instructions. Embroider French knots for the bubbles escaping from the glasses.

GIRLS INCORPORATED, LYNN RICHARDS

Fuse motifs of girls to the background. Secure three-dimensional stars with star spangles and seed beads.

REBECCA WAT

Enlarge 200% for 8" block,
225% for 9" block,
250% for 10" block,
275% for 11" block,
and 300% for 12" block.
See pages 82–83 for template and piecing instructions. Refer to *Fantastic Fabric Folding* for more detailed instructions.

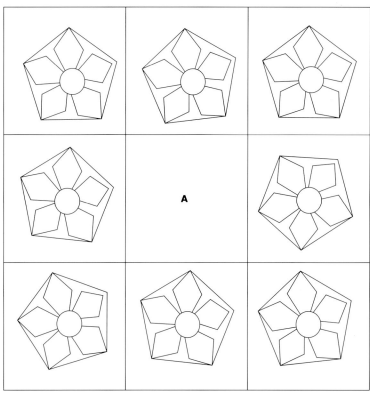

COSABETH PARRIAUD

MARIE-CHRISTINE FLOCARD

Enlarge 200% for 8" block,
225% for 9" block,
250% for 10" block,
275% for 11" block,
and 300% for 12" block.
See pages 82–83 for template
and piecing instructions.

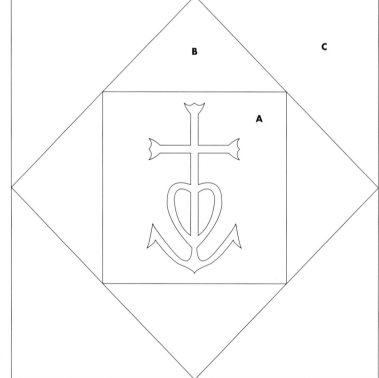

LOUISA SMITH

Enlarge 200% for 8" block,
225% for 9" block,
250% for 10" block,
275% for 11" block,
and 300% for 12" block.
Refer to *Strips 'n Curves* for more
information. See pages 82–83 for
template and piecing instructions.

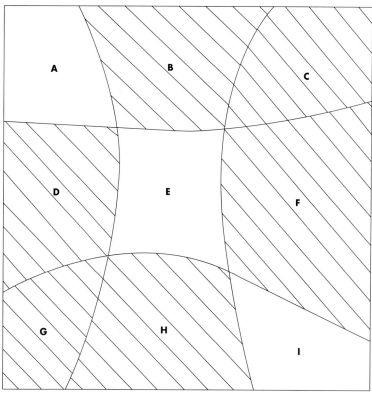

LARRAINE SCOULER

Enlarge 200% for 8" block, 225% for 9" block, 250% for 10" block, 275% for 11" block, and 300% for 12" block. See pages 82-83 for template and piecing instructions.

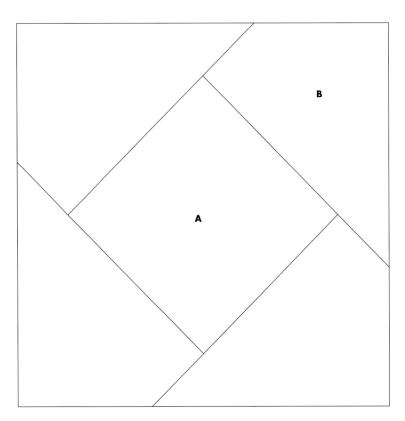

KATHY SANDBACH

Enlarge 200% for 8" block, 225% for 9" block, 250% for 10" block, 275% for 11" block, and 300% for 12" block. Refer to *Show Me How to Machine Quilt* for more detailed instructions.

CYNDY RYMER

Enlarge 200% for 8" block, 225% for 9" block, 250% for 10" block, 275% for 11" block, and 300% for 12" block. See page 83 for template and piecing instructions.

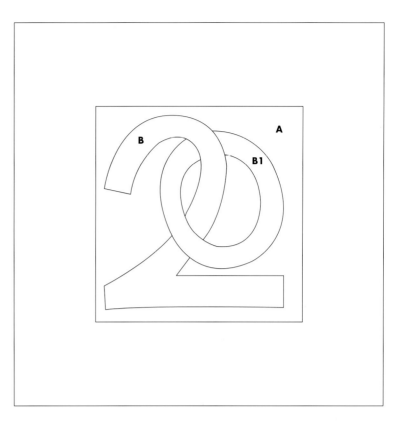

JAN KRENTZ

Enlarge 200% for 8" block, 225% for 9" block, 250% for 10" block, 275% for 11" block, and 300% for 12" block. See pages 82–83 for template and piecing instructions. Optional: Paper piece in sections, then sew sections together.

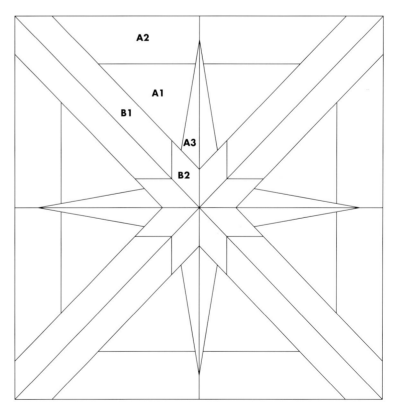

JENNIFER ROUNDS

Enlarge 200% for 8" block,

225% for 9" block,

250% for 10" block,

275% for 11" block,

and 300% for 12" block.

See pages 82–83 for template and

piecing instructions. Sew strips together

into sets, then cut equal-width ségments

for mosaic strips.

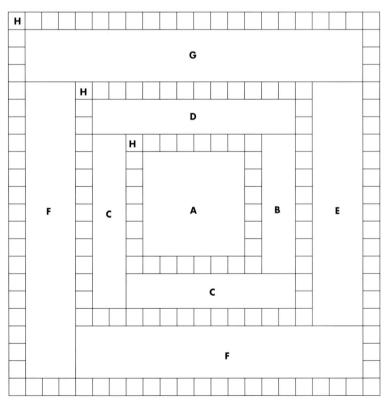

CLAUDIA OLSON

Enlarge 200% for 8" block, 225% for 9" block, 250% for 10" block, 275% for 11" block, and 300% for 12" block. See page 82–83 for template and piecing instructions.

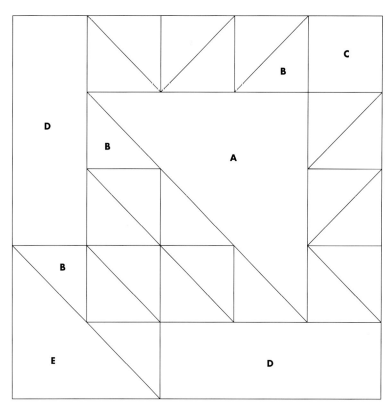

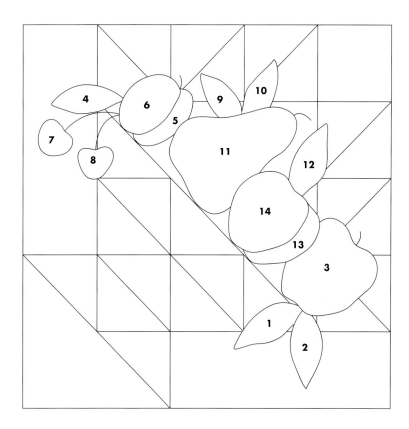

LINDA TAYLOR

Enlarge 200% for 8" block,
225% for 9" block,
250% for 10" block,
275% for 11" block,
and 300% for 12" block.
See page 83 for template and piecing
instructions. Refer to *The Ultimate Guide
to Longarm Machine Quilting* for more
detailed instructions.

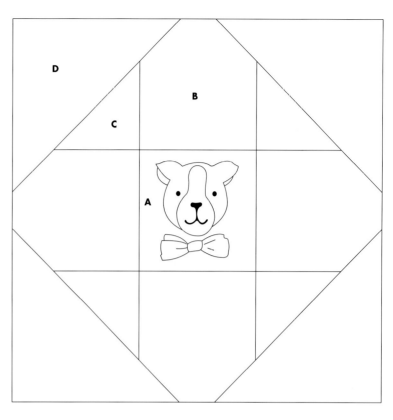

TRICE BOERENS

Enlarge 200% for 8" block, 225% for 9" block, 250% for 10" block, 275% for 11" block, and 300% for 12" block. Refer to *Quick Quilts for the Holidays* for stenciling and painting techniques. See pages 82-83 for template and piecing instructions.

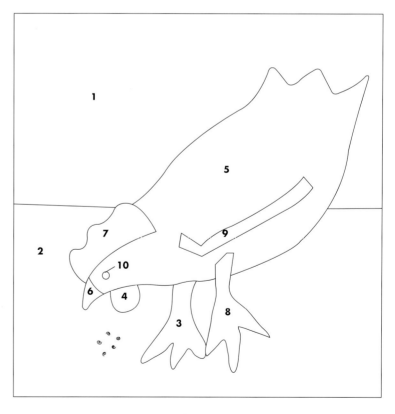

KRISTINA BECKER

Enlarge 200% for 8" block, 225% for 9" block, 250% for 10" block, 275% for 11" block, and 300% for 12" block. See page 83 for template and piecing instructions. Embroider French knots for chicken feed.

NANCY ODOM

Enlarge 200% for 8" block, 225% for 9" block, 250% for 10" block, 275% for 11" block, and 300% for 12" block. See pages 82–83 for template and piecing instructions.

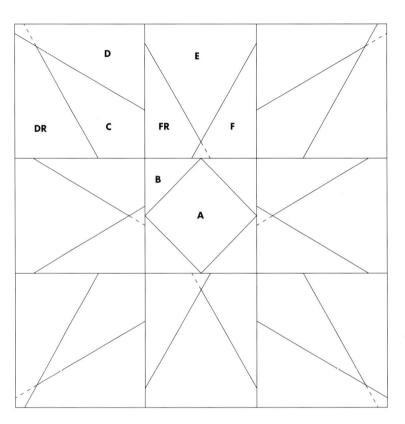

LERLENE NEVARIL

Enlarge 200% for 8" block, 225% for 9" block, 250% for 10" block, 275% for 11" block, and 300% for 12" block. See pages 82–83 for template and piecing instructions.

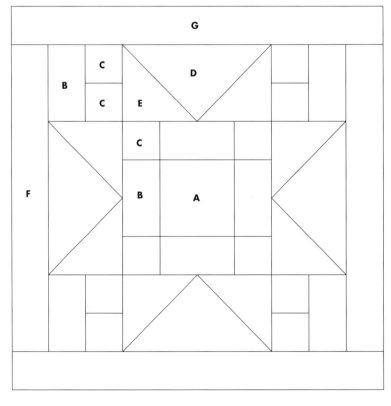

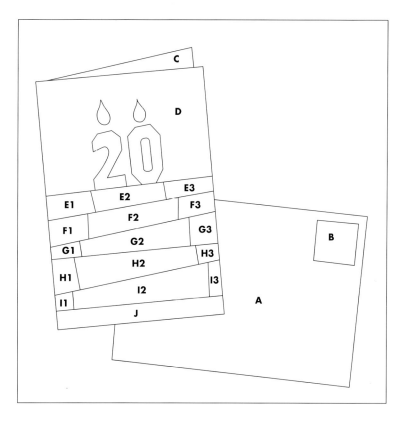

LYNETTE YOUNG BINGHAM

Enlarge 200% for 8" block, 225% for 9" block, 250% for 10" block, 275% for 11" block, and 300% for 12" block. See pages 82–83 for template and piecing instructions.

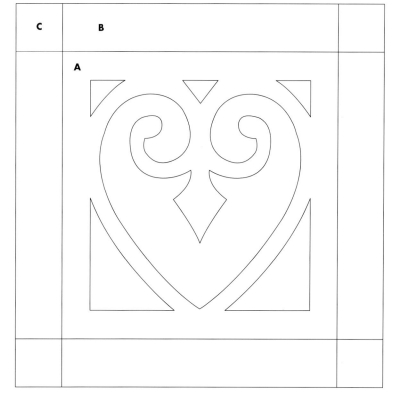

DILYS A. FRONKS

Enlarge 200% for 8" block, 225% for 9" block, 250% for 10" block, 275% for 11" block, and 300% for 12" block. See pages 82–83 for template and piecing instructions. You may find it helpful to make a small cut with scissors in the center of the holes to be cut away. This will make it easier to get the point of the scissors into the foreground fabric when the layers are basted together.

GWEN MARSTON

Enlarge 200% for 8" block,
225% for 9" block,
250% for 10" block,
275% for 11" block,
and 300% for 12" block.
See pages 82–83 for template
and piecing instructions.

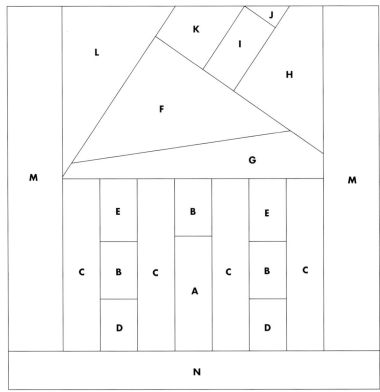

BECKY GOLDSMITH

Enlarge 200% for 8" block,
225% for 9" block,
250% for 10" block,
275% for 11" block,
and 300% for 12" block.
See page 83 for template
and piecing instructions.

LAWRY THORN

Enlarge 200% for 8" block, 225% for 9" block,
250% for 10" block, 275% for 11" block, and
300% for 12" block. See pages 82–83 for
template and piecing instructions.

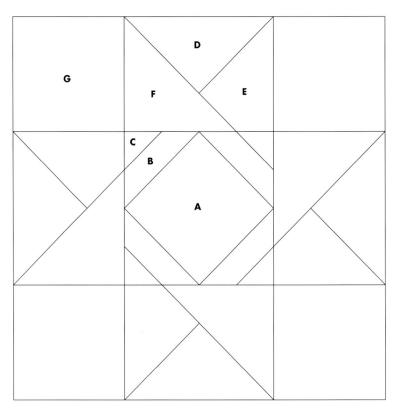

LIZ ANELOSKI

Enlarge 200% for 8" block, 225% for 9" block,
250% for 10" block, 275% for 11" block, and 300%
for 12" block. See pages 82–83 for template and
piecing instructions. Refer to *Simple Fabric Folding
for Christmas* for more detailed instructions.

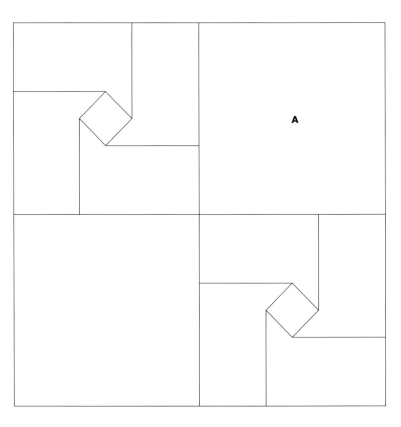

JOYCE R. BECKER

Enlarge 200% for 8" block,
225% for 9" block,
250% for 10" block,
275% for 11" block,
and 300% for 12" block.
See page 83 for template and piecing
instructions. Machine zigzag or straight
stitch the implication of smaller sky-
scrapers on the hillside in the distance.

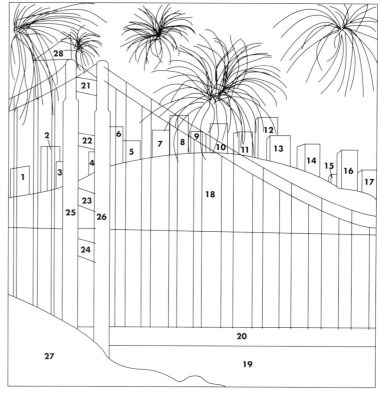

BARBARA BARBER

Enlarge 200% for 8" block,
225% for 9" block,
250% for 10" block,
275% for 11" block,
and 300% for 12" block.
See pages 82–83 for template and
piecing instructions. Refer to *Foolproof
Curves* for more detailed
instructions.

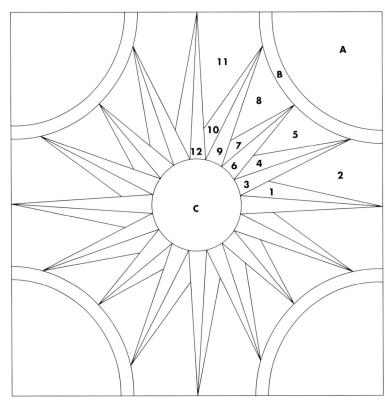

FLAVIN GLOVER

Enlarge 200% for 8" block,
225% for 9" block,
250% for 10" block,
275% for 11" block,
and 300% for 12" block.
See pages 82–83 for template and
piecing instructions. Refer to *A New
Look at Log Cabin Quilts* for more
information.

ALICE DUNSDON

Enlarge 200% for 8" block, 225% for 9" block, 250% for
10" block, 275% for 11" block, and 300% for 12" block.
See pages 82–83 for template and piecing instructions.

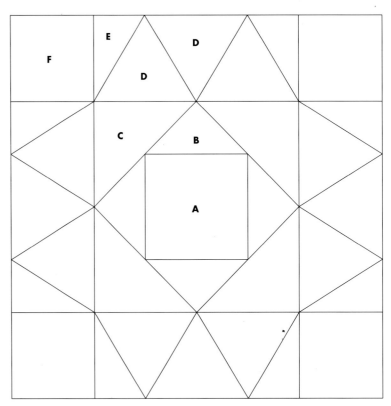

ANITA GROSSMAN SOLOMAN

Enlarge 200% for 8" block, 225% for 9" block, 250% for
10" block, 275% for 11" block, and 300% for 12" block.
See pages 82–83 for template and piecing instructions.

PEGGY MARTIN

Enlarge 200% for 8" block,

225% for 9" block,

250% for 10" block,

275% for 11" block,

and 300% for 12" block.

See pages 82–83 for template and piecing instructions. Refer to *Quick-Strip Paper Piecing* for more detailed instructions. Paper piece the arc of points in four sections, then sew the sections together to complete the circle of points.

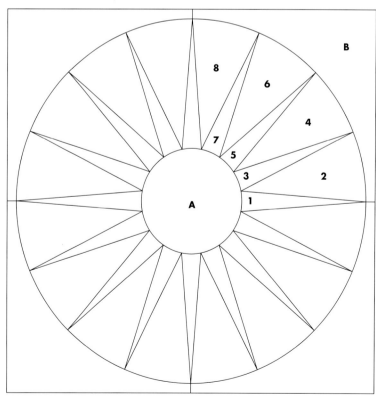

MARY LEMAN AUSTIN

Enlarge 200% for 8" block,
225% for 9" block,
250% for 10" block,
275% for 11" block,
and 300% for 12" block.
See pages 82–83 for template
and piecing instructions.

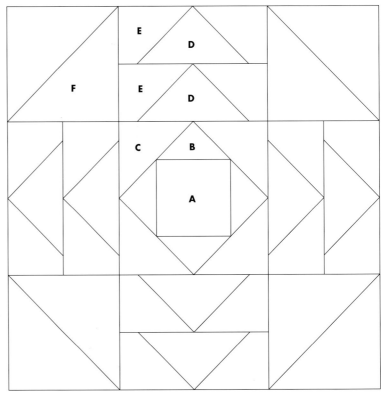

CELEBRATING 20 YEARS

OF EXTRAORDINARY AUTHORS

AND ENDLESS INSPIRATION

List of Authors AND THEIR BOOKS

CHARLOTTE WARR ANDERSEN
Faces & Places
Focus on Features

ALEX ANDERSON
Beautifully Quilted with Alex Anderson
Fabric Shopping with Alex Anderson
Hand Appliqué with Alex Anderson
Hand Quilting with Alex Anderson
Kids Start Quilting with Alex Anderson
Paper Piecing with Alex Anderson
Quilts for Fabric Lovers
Rotary Cutting with Alex Anderson
Shadow Redwork™ with Alex Anderson
Simply Stars
Start Quilting with Alex Anderson
Start Quilting with Alex Anderson, 2nd Edition
Stars Galore Gift Wrap
Star Quilts Notecards
Basket Quilt Pattern
Double Sawtooth Star Pattern
Nine-Patch Variation Pattern
Rail Fence with Stars Pattern
Redwork Pillow Shams Pattern
Redwork Quilt Pattern
Shadow Redwork Fruit Quilt Pattern

LIZ ANELOSKI
Simple Fabric Folding for Christmas
Stamped Drunkard's Path Pattern

LIZ ANELOSKI & JOYCE LYTLE
Celebrate the Tradition

LIZ ANELOSKI & KANDY PETERSEN
Quick & Easy Block Tool

CAROL ARMSTRONG
Appliqué Inside the Lines
Butterflies & Blooms
Cats in Quilts
Quilting with Carol Armstrong
Wild Birds
Wildflowers
Wildflower Notecards

Double Wedding Ring Pattern
Rosie, Queen of the Roses Pattern

MARY LEMAN AUSTIN
QNM: The First 35 Years

VIRGINIA AVERY
Hats: A Heady Affair
Nifty Neckwear

MIMI AYARS & PATRICIA B. CAMPBELL
Jacobean Rhapsodies
Jacobean Notecards

COZY BAKER
Kaleidoscope Artistry
Kaleidoscopes

BARBARA BARBER
Foolproof Curves

AMY BARICKMAN
Forever Yours

JOYCE R. BECKER
Luscious Landscapes

KRISTINA BECKER
Come Listen to My Quilts

SUE BEEVERS
Free-Form Painted Fabric

JINNY BEYER
Soft-Edge Piecing

LYNETTE YOUNG BINGHAM & BLANCHE YOUNG
Dresden Flower Garden

TRICE BOERENS
Quick Quilts for the Holidays

PAM BONO DESIGNS
Quilt It for Kids

BARBARA BRACKMAN
Civil War Women
Quilts from the Civil War
Quilts: Making History

CHERYL GREIDER BRADKIN
Basic Seminole Patchwork

KAREY BRESENHAN
America from the Heart

LAUREL BURCH
Laurel Burch Christmas, A
Laurel Burch Quilts
Kindred Creatures Gift Wrap
Kindred Creatures Notecards
Folkloric Flutter-byes Quilt Pattern

LAUREL BURCH & CYNDY LYLE RYMER
Mythical Dogs Pattern

PATRICIA B. CAMPBELL & MIMI AYARS
Jacobean Rhapsodies
Jacobean Notecards

SUSAN CARLSON
Free-Style Quilts

JENNIFER CHIAVERINI & NANCY ODOM
Elm Creek Quilts

DARLENE C. CHRISTOPHERSON
Perfect Union of Patchwork & Appliqué, A

KIM CHURBUCK
Create Your Own Quilt Labels!
Art of Machine Piecing, The
Small Scale Quiltmaking
Quilt Block Sampler Gift Wrap

CATHERINE COMYNS & JENNIFER ROUNDS
A Floral Affair

SALLY COLLINS
Small Scale Quiltmaking
Art of Machine Piecing, The

PEPPER CORY
Crosspatch
Happy Trails
Mastering Quilt Marking
Quilting Designs from Antique Quilts
Quilting Designs from the Amish

SHARYN CRAIG
Setting Solutions

SHARYN CRAIG & HARRIET HARGRAVE
Art of Classic Quiltmaking, The

NANCY CROW
Nancy Crow: Improvisational Quilts

SANDI CUMMINGS
Beyond the Block

JUDY B. DALES
Curves in Motion

SUSAN DELANEY-MECH
Rx for Quilters

KRISTEN DIBBS
Machine Embroidery and More

BETH DONALDSON & MARSHA MacDOWELL
Fanny's Fan Quilt Pattern

ALICE DUNSDON
Fantastic Fans

MARIE-CHRISTINE FLOCARD & COSABETH PARRIAUD
Provence Quilts and Cuisine
Tote Bag Pattern

MARIANNE FONS
Fine Feathers

MARIANNE FONS & LIZ PORTER
Let's Make Waves

DIANE C. FRANKENBERGER & KRISTIN C. STEINER
At Piece With Time

ANN FRISCHKORN & AMY SANDRIN
Flower Pounding

LAURA LEE FRITZ
250 Continuous-Line Quilting Designs
250 More Continuous-Line Quilting Designs

DILYS A. FRONKS
Enchanted Views

HELEN YOUNG FROST & BLANCHE YOUNG
Boston Commons Quilt, The
Flying Geese Quilt, The
Irish Chain Quilts
New Lone Star Quilt Handbook, The
Trip Around the World Quilts

JENNIFER GILBERT
New England Quilt Museum Quilts, The

GIRLS INCORPORATED
Women of Taste

FLAVIN GLOVER
New Look at Log Cabin Quilts, A

BECKY GOLDSMITH & LINDA JENKINS
Contemporary Classics in Plaids & Stripes
Flowering Favorites from Piece O' Cake Designs
Slice of Christmas from Piece O' Cake Designs, A
Festive Florals Gift Wrap
Lucky Stars Pattern

MIRIAM GOURLEY
Whimsical Animals

JEFFREY GUTCHEON
Diamond Patchwork

JANE HALL & DIXIE HAYWOOD
Perfect Pineapples

GLORIA HANSEN
Free Stuff for Pet Lovers on the Internet
Free Stuff for Traveling Quilters on the Internet

GLORIA HANSEN & JUDY HEIM

Free Stuff for Collectors on the Internet
Free Stuff for Crafty Kids on the Internet
Free Stuff for Doll Lovers on the Internet
Free Stuff for Gardeners on the Internet
Free Stuff for Home Décor on the Internet
Free Stuff for Home Repair on the Internet
Free Stuff for Quilters on the Internet
Free Stuff for Quilters on the Internet, 2nd Edition
Free Stuff for Quilters on the Internet, 3rd Edition
Free Stuff for Sewing Fanatics on the Internet
Free Stuff for Stitchers on the Internet

HARRIET HARGRAVE

From Fiber to Fabric
Heirloom Machine Quilting, 2nd Edition
Heirloom Machine Quilting, Third Edition
Mastering Machine Appliqué
Mastering Machine Appliqué, 2nd Edition
Quick-Look Guide: Caring for Fabric & Quilts
Quick-Look Guide: Choosing Batting
Classic Quilts Notecards
Heirloom Quilts Notecards
Christmas Lily Pattern
Oriental Poppy Pattern

HARRIET HARGRAVE & SHARYN CRAIG

Art of Classic Quiltmaking, The

DIXIE HAYWOOD & JANE HALL

Perfect Pineapples

VALERIE HEARDER

Beyond the Horizon

JUDY HEIM & GLORIA HANSEN

Free Stuff for Collectors on the Internet
Free Stuff for Crafty Kids on the Internet
Free Stuff for Doll Lovers on the Internet
Free Stuff for Gardeners on the Internet
Free Stuff for Home Décor on the Internet
Free Stuff for Home Repair on the Internet
Free Stuff for Quilters on the Internet
Free Stuff for Quilters on the Internet, 2nd Edition
Free Stuff for Quilters on the Internet, 3rd Edition
Free Stuff for Sewing Fanatics on the Internet
Free Stuff for Stitchers on the Internet

CAROLIE HENSLEY

Log Cabin Quilt Pattern

THE JIM HENSON COMPANY IN ASSOCIATION WITH THE SESAME WORKSHOP

Quilting with the Muppets
Muppets Quilts Gift Wrap
Quilted Muppets Notecards

WENDY HILL

On the Surface
Two-For-One Foundation Piecing

JULIE HIROTA

Subtractive Appliqué

ROBERTA HORTON

An Amish Adventure
An Amish Adventure, 2nd Edition
Calico and Beyond
Fabric Makes the Quilt, The
Plaids & Stripes
Scrap Quilts
Stained Glass Quilting Technique
Country Quilts Gift Wrap
Amish Notecards, 2nd Edition
Amish Quilts Notecards
Scrap Quilts Notecards

RITA HUTCHENS

Totally Tubular Quilts

MICHAEL JAMES

Michael James: Art & Inspirations
Studio Quilts Notecards

LINDA JENKINS & BECKY GOLDSMITH

Contemporary Classics in Plaids & Stripes
Flowering Favorites from Piece O' Cake Designs
Slice of Christmas from Piece O' Cake Designs, A
Festive Florals Gift Wrap
Lucky Stars Pattern

LYNETTE JENSEN

Cozy Cabin Quilts from Thimbleberries
Thimbleberries Housewarming, A
Thimbleberries Gift Wrap
Thimbleberries Classics Gift Wrap
Quilts from Thimbleberries Notecards
Thimbleberries Favorites Notecards

LINDA JOHANSEN

Fast, Fun & Easy Fabric Bowls

NANCY JOHNSON-SREBRO

Block Magic
Block Magic, Too!
Endless Possibilities

JUDITH BAKER MONTANO
Art of Silk Ribbon Embroidery, The
Crazy Quilt Handbook, The
Crazy Quilt Handbook, The, 2nd Edition
Crazy Quilt Odyssey
Elegant Stitches
Floral Stitches
Judith Baker Montano: Art & Inspirations
Recollections
Victorian Romance Gift Wrap
Elegant Stitches Notecards
Keepsake Recollections Notecards
Memories Notecards
Seascapes Notecards
Victorian Family Notecards
Victorian Medley Notecards
Victorian Pansies Notecards
Victorian Recollections Notecards
Judith Baker Montano's Crazy Quilting Video
Judith Baker Montano's Silk Ribbon Embroidery Video
Judith Montano's Embellishments Video
Judith Montano's Landscapes Video

FREDDY MORAN
Freddy's House
House Party Quilts Gift Wrap
Quilted Houses Notecards

JAN MULLEN
Cut-Loose Quilts
Reverse Appliqué with No Brakez

PAULA NADELSTERN
Kaleidoscopes & Quilts
Snowflakes & Quilts
Kaleidoscope Quilts Gift Wrap
Kaleidoscopic Quilts Notecards
Quilted Snowflakes Notecards

LERLENE NEVARIL
Hidden Block Quilts

VELDA E. NEWMAN
Workshop with Velda Newman, A

SHIRLEY NILSSON
Stitching Free

LAURA NOWNES & DIANA McCLUN
Q is for Quilt
Quilts, Quilts, and More Quilts!
Say It with Quilts
Quilter's Delight Gift Wrap
Quilts, Quilts & More Quilts Notecards
Say It With Quilts Notecards
Alphabet Sampler Pattern

Hearts Quilt Pattern
Kid Prints Quilt Pattern
Molly's Magic Pansies Pattern

NANCY ODOM
Joanna's Pumpkins & Pomegranates Pattern

NANCY ODOM & JENNIFER CHIAVERINI
Elm Creek Quilts

OKLAHOMA EMBROIDERY SUPPLY & DESIGN
Sew Much Fun

CELIA Y. OLIVER
Enduring Grace
Enduring Grace Notecards

CLAUDIA OLSON
15 Two-Block Quilts
Twice as Nice Gift Wrap

ONDORI STAFF
Book of Patchwork from Japan

SUSANNA OROYAN
Anatomy of a Doll
Designing the Doll
Dolls of the Art Deco Era, 1910–1940
Fantastic Figures
Finishing the Figure

KATHY PACE
Best From Gooseberry Hill, The

REYNOLA PAKUSICH
Circles

COSABETH PARRIAUD & MARIE-CHRISTINE FLOCARD
Provence Quilts and Cuisine
Tote Bag Pattern

KATIE PASQUINI MASOPUST
3-Dimensional Design
Contemporary Sampler
Fractured Landscape Quilts
Ghost Layers and Color Washes
Isometric Perspective
Mandala

CHARLOTTE PATERA
Schoolhouse Appliqué

GAI PERRY
24 Quilted Gems
Color from the Heart
Do-It-Yourself Framed Quilts
Impressionist Palette
Impressionist Quilts
Color in Quilts Gift Wrap
Quilted Treasures Gift Wrap
All About Color Notecards

Impressionist Palette Notecards
Impressionist Quilts Notecards

MARGARET PETERS
Christmas Traditions from the Heart 1
Christmas Traditions from the Heart 2
I'll Be Home for Christmas Pattern

KANDY PETERSEN & LIZ ANELOSKI
Quick & Easy Block Tool

DIANE PHALEN
Diane Phalen Quilts
Celebrate the Seasons Notecards
Country Scenes Notecards
Tulips in a Vase Pattern

YVONNE PORCELLA
Colorful Book, A
Colors Changing Hue
Magical Four-Patch and Nine-Patch Quilts
Pieced Clothing
Pieced Clothing Variations
Six Color World
Yvonne Porcella: Art & Inspirations
Colorful Quilts Notecards

LIZ PORTER & MARIANNE FONS
Let's Make Waves

QUILT SAN DIEGO
Visions: Layers of Excellence
Visions: QuiltArt
Visions: Quilts of a New Decade
Visions: The Art of the Quilt

QUILTER'S NEWSLETTER MAGAZINE & QUILTMAKER
All About Quilting from A to Z
Paper Piecing Potpourri
Paper Piecing Picnic

JAN RAPACZ
Teddy Bear Redwork

RUTH REYNOLDS
RIVA

JENNIFER ROUNDS & CATHERINE COMYNS
Floral Affair, A

JENNIFER ROUNDS & CYNDY LYLE RYMER
Bouquet of Quilts, A
Wine Country Quilts

CYNDY LYLE RYMER
Quilts for Guys
Shoreline Quilts

CYNDY RYMER & LAUREL BURCH
Mythical Dogs Pattern

CYNDY LYLE RYMER & JENNIFER ROUNDS
Bouquet of Quilts, A

Wine Country Quilts

JENNIFER SAMPOU & CAROLYN SCHMITZ
In the Nursery
Little Red Hen Pattern

KATHY SANDBACH
Show Me How to Machine Quilt

AMY SANDRIN & ANN FRISCHKORN
Flower Pounding

JANE A. SASSAMAN
Quilted Garden, The
Textile Gardens Notecards

BECKY SCHAEFER
Working in Miniature

DEIDRE SCHERER
Deidre Scherer
Still Life Notecards

CAROLYN SCHMITZ & JENNIFER SAMPOU
In the Nursery
Little Red Hen Pattern

LARRAINE SCOULER
Quilting Back to Front

ELLY SIENKIEWICZ
Appliqué 12 Borders and Medallions
Appliqué 12 Easy Ways!
Appliqué 12 Easy Ways, 2nd Edition
Baltimore Album Legacy
Baltimore Album Quilts
Baltimore Album Revival!
Baltimore Beauties and Beyond Vol. 1
Baltimore Beauties and Beyond Vol. 2
Best of Baltimore Beauties, The
Best of Baltimore Beauties Part II, The
Design A Baltimore Album Quilt!
Dimensional Appliqué
Fancy Appliqué
Papercuts and Plenty
Sweet Dreams, Moon Baby
Fancy Appliqué Notecards

DONNA INGRAM SLUSSER
Rainbow Stars Quilt Pattern

DONNA INGRAM SLUSSER & PATRICIA MAIXNER MAGARET
Shadow Quilts
Shadows Notecards

LOUISA L. SMITH
Strips 'n Curves

NANCY SMITH & LYNDA MILLIGAN
Plentiful Possibilities

ANITA GROSSMAN SOLOMON
Make it Simpler Paper Piecing

DOREEN SPECKMANN
Pattern Play
Travels with Peaky and Spike
Ambrosia Quilt Pattern

KRISTIN C. STEINER & DIANE C. FRANKENBERGER
At Piece With Time

DALENE YOUNG STONE & BLANCHE YOUNG
Tradition with a Twist

TERRELL SUNDERMANN
Pieced Roman Shades

LINDA V. TAYLOR
Ultimate Guide to Longarm Machine Quilting, The

LAWRY THORN & JEAN WELLS
Four Seasons in Flannel

RICKY TIMS
Ricky Tims' Convergence Quilts

HARI WALNER
Exploring Machine Trapunto
Trapunto by Machine

REBECCA WAT
Fantastic Fabric Folding
Springtime Impression I Quilt Pattern
Springtime Impression II Quilt Pattern

MARY LOU WEIDMAN
Quilted Memories

JEAN WELLS
Buttonhole Stitch Appliqué
Fans
Memorabilia Quilting
Patchwork Quilts Made Easy
Patchwork Quilts Made Easy - Revised, 2nd Edition
Willowood
No Sew Appliqué: Bloomin' Creations
No Sew Appliqué: Fans, Hearts and Folk Art
No Sew Appliqué: Holiday Magic
No Sew Appliqué: Hometown
PQME I: Milky Way
PQME I: Nine Patch
PQME I: Pinwheel
PQME I: Stars and Hearts
PQME II: The Basket Quilt
PQME II: The Bear's Paw Quilt
PQME II: The Country Bunny Quilt
PQME II: The Sawtooth Star Quilt
Quilts in the Garden Notecards
Willowood Notecards
Lettuce in the Garden Quilt Pattern
Patchwork Quilts Made Easy Video

JEAN WELLS & MARINA ANDERSON
Celebration of Hearts, A
Picture This

JEAN WELLS & LAWRY THORN
Four Seasons in Flannel

JEAN & VALORI WELLS
Along the Garden Path
Everything Flowers
Garden-Inspired Quilts
Through the Garden Gate
Floral Fancy Gift Wrap
Garden Quilts Notecards

VALORI WELLS
Radiant New York Beauties
Stitch 'n Flip Quilts
Radiant Beauties Gift Wrap

VALORI & JEAN WELLS
Along the Garden Path
Everything Flowers
Garden-Inspired Quilts
Through the Garden Gate
Floral Fancy Gift Wrap
Garden Quilts Notecards

JOEN WOLFROM
Color Play
Landscapes and Illusions
Magical Effects of Color, The
Make Any Block Any Size
Patchwork Persuasion
Seasonal Projects
Visual Dance, The
Patchwork Persuasion Notecards
Spring is Sprung Pattern
3-in-1 Color Tool
3-in-1 Color Tool, Revised

BLANCHE YOUNG
Radiant Nine Patch

BLANCHE YOUNG & DALENE YOUNG STONE
Tradition with a Twist

BLANCHE YOUNG & HELEN YOUNG FROST
Boston Commons Quilt, The
Flying Geese Quilt, The
Irish Chain Quilts
New Lone Star Quilt Handbook, The
Trip Around the World Quilts

BLANCHE YOUNG & LYNETTE YOUNG BINGHAM
Dresden Flower Garden

Index

Other fine books from C&T Publishing

For more information, ask for a free catalog:
C&T Publishing, Inc.
P.O. Box 1456
Lafayette, CA 94549
(800) 284-1114
Email: ctinfo@ctpub.com
Website: www.ctpub.com

For quilting supplies:
Cotton Patch Mail Order
3405 Hall Lane, Dept.CTB
Lafayette, CA 94549
(800) 835-4418
(925) 283-7883
Email: quiltusa@yahoo.com
Website: www.quiltusa.com